Your First Home Unlocked

Build Your Deposit Faster, Secure the Right Mortgage, and Buy with Confidence Without Waiting for the Bank of Mum and Dad

Anthony Fallon, AssocRICS

Anthony Fallon Publishing

First edition 2026

ISBN's
978-1-918189-10-0 eBook
978-1-918189-11-7 Paperback
978-1-918189-12-4 Hardback

A CIP Catalogue record for this book is available from the British Library. Copies of the book have been deposited with the UK Legal Deposit system at the following:
National Library of Scotland
The Bodleian Library, University of Oxford
National Library of Wales
Cambridge University Library
The Library of Trinity College Dublin

Contents

Introduction: The Knowledge You Were Never Given

At 2am on a Tuesday, Carina refreshed Rightmove for the forty-seventh time that week. She'd been renting in Manchester for eight years, earning £38,000 as a marketing manager, and the maths hadn't changed since she started looking six months ago. The two-bedroom terrace she could just about afford had jumped from £185,000 to £198,000 in that time, while her deposit savings account had crept from £14,200 to £16,800. At this rate, house prices would outpace her savings forever, and she'd still be renting at 40, scrolling property portals in the dark whilst her university friends posted Instagram stories from their housewarming parties.

Carina isn't failing. The game was rigged from the start.

You know this feeling because you're living it. You're 32, or 35, or 38, and you've done everything right, degree completed, career progressing, debt managed responsibly, yet homeownership feels further away now than it did five years ago. You watch colleagues who received £40,000 deposits from parents buy three-bedroom houses in desirable postcodes whilst you're still calculating whether cutting your coffee budget will shave three months or six months off your timeline. You've read the articles, listened to the podcasts, consulted the mortgage calculators, and somehow feel less confident than when you started. The more you research, the more paralysed you become.

Here's what nobody's telling you: buying your first home was never about what you could afford, it was always about what you knew.

The Real Barrier Isn't Your Salary

Let me show you two buyers. Both are 34 years old, both earn £36,000 annually, both live in Birmingham, and both started with £12,000 in savings. Neither received parental help.

Buyer A spent two years researching. She read every first-time buyer guide, joined three Facebook groups, consulted four mortgage comparison websites, and viewed 37 properties. She eventually bought a two-bedroom flat for £165,000 after 31 months of active searching. By the time she completed, the combination of arrangement fees, survey costs, overpaying for the property (she'd become emotionally attached after the third viewing), and accepting a mortgage product with a 3.8% rate because she didn't understand the true cost structure had added approximately £34,000 to her total homeownership cost over five years.

Buyer B spent six weeks learning a structured system. She understood precisely which government schemes applied to her situation, implemented an automated deposit acceleration plan, secured an Agreement in Principle 60 days before viewing properties, used a five-criteria filter to eliminate unsuitable options within minutes, and completed on a two-bedroom house for £168,000 after 14 months total timeline. She secured a mortgage at 3.1%, avoided every catastrophic mistake checkpoint, and reached completion with her emergency fund intact.

The difference between these two buyers wasn't intelligence, work ethic, or luck. It was structured knowledge applied systematically.

Buyer A had more information, thousands of forum posts, dozens of articles, conflicting expert opinions. Buyer B had the right knowledge at the right time in the right sequence. Information overwhelms. Knowledge liberates.

The UK Housing Market Is an Information Asymmetry Problem

We've been sold a lie about the UK housing crisis. The dominant narrative positions it purely as an affordability problem: house prices have outpaced wage growth, deposits are impossibly large, and unless you have the "Bank of Mum and Dad," you're locked out forever. This narrative is emotionally satisfying because it removes your agency, if the system is broken and you can't change the system, then your paralysis is rational, even noble.

But here's the uncomfortable truth: successful first-time buyers without parental help exist at every income level between £30,000 and £60,000 across every major UK city. They're completing in London on £40,000 salaries, in Manchester on £33,000, in Bristol on £37,000, in Edinburgh on £35,000. They're not earning dramatically more than you. They're not getting secret windfalls. They're not working three jobs or living with their parents until 35.

What differentiates them is access to three things you haven't had:

1. Precise baseline truth about their exact financial position, not vague estimates

2. Protection-first knowledge about the six decision nodes where lack of information causes irreversible damage

3. Sequential implementation architecture that converts paralysis into momentum

The UK property market operates as a generational wealth transfer mechanism disguised as a meritocracy. Those with parental deposits skip the entire accumulation phase and enter the market with structural advantages, larger deposits, better mortgage rates, more negotiating power, faster timelines. Those without parental help face a secondary barrier that's rarely discussed: the information asymmetry that silently costs unprepared buyers £30,000-£50,000 and extends timelines by 3-5 years.

You already suspected the financial system was rigged. What you didn't know is that the information environment was just as broken, and unlike the financial system, the information problem has a solution you can control.

Your Paralysis Is Rational. Your Liberation Is Possible.

If you're feeling paralysed right now, that's not a character flaw, it's an intelligent response to a genuinely confusing environment. You've been researching for months, maybe years, and the effect has been paradoxical: the more you learn, the less confident you feel. This pattern has a name in behavioural economics, information overload leading to decision paralysis, and it's structural, not personal.

Here's what's actually happening. The UK first-time buyer information environment consists of:

- Government schemes with eligibility criteria that change annually

- 3,000+ mortgage products with varying fee structures, early repayment charges, and true cost calculations

- Property types with hidden risks (leasehold ground rent escalation, cladding compliance, EPC requirements)

- Regional markets with different price-to-income ratios requiring different strategies

- Legal processes with undefined timelines and coordination requirements

- Conflicting expert advice optimised for clicks, not your specific situation

You've been trying to navigate this complexity without a map, without a sequence, without protection checkpoints, and without any way to distinguish signal from noise. The result is predictable: you've absorbed enormous amounts of information whilst building zero confidence in your ability to make good decisions.

But here's the truth that changes everything: buying your first home without parental help is entirely achievable at your income level. The missing ingredient isn't higher earnings, better luck, or perfect timing. It's structured knowledge applied systematically through a protection-first framework designed specifically for your income bracket, your city, and your constraints.

The Renter Liberation System: Your Operating System for Homeownership

This book introduces the only complete operating system built specifically for first time buying without family support: **The Renter Liberation System**.

It's structured around a six-stage framework that does something unusual, it turns your current identity into the very process that dissolves it. The framework is called **RENTER**:

- **Reveal**, Uncover Your True Financial Starting Point
- **Engineer**, Build Your 18-Month Financial Runway
- **Navigate**, Master Mortgages and Maximise Your Borrowing Power
- **Target**, Identify, Evaluate, and Select the Right Property
- **Execute**, Make Your Offer, Protect the Deal, and Complete
- **Reside**, Transition Successfully Into Proud, Solvent Homeownership

Each stage builds irreversible forward momentum toward the next. You can't engineer an 18-month financial runway until you've revealed your precise baseline. You can't navigate mortgages effectively until you know your exact deposit target date. You can't target properties strategically until you have your Agreement in Principle secured. The sequence matters because each stage eliminates one layer of paralysis and replaces it with structured action.

This isn't another collection of disconnected tips. This is an integrated operating system where every component works together by design, built on a single philosophical foundation: preventing catastrophic mistakes is worth more than optimising gains.

The system is protection-first because that's what you actually need. You don't need to find the absolute perfect property at the absolute perfect price with the absolute perfect mortgage, you need to avoid the leasehold nightmare with escalating ground rent, the cladding disaster that makes your flat un-mortgageable, the survey red flag you ignored because you'd already fallen in love with the kitchen, the mortgage product with a 5% early repayment charge that traps you for five years.

Every stage includes explicit go/no-go decision checkpoints. You'll know exactly when to proceed, when to renegotiate, and when to walk away. You'll never again confuse gut feeling with strategic judgment.

The Three-Part Journey Ahead

This book is structured in three parts, each with a specific purpose:

Part I: (Chapters 1-4) dismantles your paralysis by revealing the true nature of the game. You'll understand why your struggle is structural, not personal. You'll discover what actually separates successful buyers from perpetual renters at identical income levels. You'll learn the complete architecture of the Renter Liberation System before implementation begins, ensuring your commitment is informed, not impulsive.

Part II: (Chapters 5-10) executes the six-stage RENTER Framework in sequence. You'll establish your precise financial baseline, design your automated 18-month deposit runway, master the mortgage landscape, install your property evaluation filter, and navigate the active purchase phase with confidence and protection. This is where paralysis converts into irreversible forward momentum.

Part III: (Chapters 11-18) extends beyond completion into the critical first year of homeownership, the phase every other resource ignores. You'll manage the post-purchase financial reset, rebuild your emergency fund, establish sustainable homeowner practices, and navigate the specific challenges of solo buyers, couples, London/South East markets, and regional cities. You'll also build resilience against major life disruptions, ensuring you remain a solvent, capable homeowner long-term.

The entire system is designed for the **5-Hour Weekend Method**, you can implement every stage whilst working 45-55 hours weekly. This respects your time poverty and eliminates the need for weekday availability or career disruption.

You Are Not the Problem

Let me be absolutely clear about something: you are not failing at homeownership.

You're not bad with money. You're not lazy. You're not stupid. You're not expecting too much. You haven't made terrible life choices. You're not less capable than your peers who own homes.

What you've been experiencing is the predictable outcome of navigating a deliberately complex system without the structured knowledge architecture that makes success inevitable rather than impossible. The UK property market rewards information access, and until now, you haven't had access to the right information in the right sequence with the right protection.

This book is the fix.

By the time you reach the final chapter, you'll have transformed from a paralysed renter who felt stupid every time you looked at Rightmove into a genuinely proud homeowner who looks back knowing you made every decision well. You'll have proven to yourself, your family, and your peers that intelligence and strategy can overcome the structural advantages you were never given.

The 18-month timeline is realistic, not fantasy. The protection framework is comprehensive, not superficial. The case studies are real buyers at your income level who succeeded using this exact system. The tools are professional-grade and ready to use. The knowledge is complete and structured for implementation.

You've spent years believing the problem was affordability. You've spent months drowning in information that only increased your paralysis. You've spent enough time doubting yourself.

It's time to start.

In Chapter 1, we'll examine exactly why your struggle to buy isn't personal failure but structural design, and why understanding this distinction is the essential first step toward liberation.

You're Not Failing, The Game Was Rigged

The UK housing market isn't broken; it's working exactly as designed.

You've been told that if you just saved harder, budgeted better, or sacrificed more, homeownership would eventually arrive. That's not true. The system you're fighting against was deliberately restructured over the past three decades to transfer wealth between generations, not reward individual effort. The proof isn't in political rhetoric or economic theory; it's in the mathematics that govern your life every single month. And those numbers reveal a simple, brutal truth: you were never meant to win this game through hard work alone. This chapter will prove it to you.

The Maths That Don't Add Up

Let's start with the arithmetic that keeps you awake at 2am, scrolling through Rightmove with a growing sense of dread.

You earn £38,000 annually in Manchester. After tax and National Insurance, that's roughly £29,500 take-home, or £2,458 per month. You've read all the advice: save 20% of your income for a deposit. So you commit £491 monthly to your Lifetime ISA. You're proud of this, it feels disciplined, responsible, like you're finally doing something right.

The median house price in Manchester is £235,000. With a 10% deposit, you need £23,500. At £491 per month, you'll reach that target in 47.9 months, just under four years. Not ideal, but achievable. You can see the finish line.

Here's what the advice never tells you: the finish line is moving faster than you are.

Manchester house prices have appreciated at an average of 8.4% annually over the past decade. That £235,000 property you're targeting? In four years, it'll cost approximately

£324,000. Your deposit requirement just jumped from £23,500 to £32,400. You haven't fallen behind because you failed to save, you've fallen behind because the asset you're chasing is appreciating faster than your savings can accumulate.

This isn't a Manchester problem. It's a structural problem embedded across every UK region. Here's what the maths looks like at different income levels and cities:

Income	City	Median Price	Annual Appreciation	Monthly Saving (20%)	Years to 10% Deposit	Price After Saving Period	New Deposit Gap
£35,000	Leeds	£215,000	7.2%	£467	4.1 years	£285,000	+£7,000
£42,000	Birmingham	£245,000	8.1%	£560	3.6 years	£322,000	+£7,700
£48,000	Bristol	£375,000	9.3%	£640	4.9 years	£540,000	+£16,500
£55,000	London (Zone 4)	£485,000	10.2%	£733	5.5 years	£800,000	+£31,500

The table reveals what you've suspected but couldn't prove: the traditional savings approach is mathematically designed to fail. The gap doesn't close; it widens. You're not climbing a ladder; you're running on a treadmill set at an incline you didn't choose and can't control.

Your salary, meanwhile, increases at roughly 2-3% annually if you're lucky, barely keeping pace with inflation, let alone house price growth. The system isn't rewarding your discipline. It's punishing your lack of inherited wealth.

When Homeownership Became an Inheritance, Not an Achievement

This wasn't always true. Your parents' generation bought their first homes in their mid-twenties on single incomes without parental help. You've heard the stories: "We saved for two years and bought a three-bedroom semi." It sounds like fiction now, but it was standard reality in 1995.

What changed?

Three policy decisions restructured the UK housing market between 1997 and 2016, transforming it from an accessible asset class into a generational wealth transfer mechanism:

1. Quantitative Easing (2009-2016): The Bank of England pumped £445 billion into the economy following the 2008 financial crisis. This liquidity didn't flow into wages or productivity, it inflated asset prices. Property became the primary beneficiary. Those who already owned property saw values skyrocket. Those who didn't own property saw the entry price move permanently out of reach.

2. Help to Buy (2013-2023): Marketed as a first-time buyer scheme, Help to Buy's actual effect was demand inflation. By allowing buyers to purchase with 5% deposits backed by government loans, the scheme increased competition for properties without increasing supply. Sellers simply raised prices to capture the artificial demand. The Resolution Foundation found that Help to Buy added an average of £8,250 to house prices, benefiting sellers and developers, not buyers.

3. Interest Rate Suppression (2009-2022): The Bank of England base rate remained below 1% for over a decade. Cheap borrowing costs allowed existing homeowners to borrow against equity, purchase second properties, and expand buy-to-let portfolios. First-time buyers without existing equity couldn't access the same capital multiplication. The wealth gap between homeowners and renters widened exponentially.

These weren't accidents. They were deliberate choices that prioritised economic stability and homeowner wealth over intergenerational fairness. And the data proves it worked, for people who already owned property.

According to the Institute for Fiscal Studies, the average homeowner aged 55-64 saw their property wealth increase by £175,000 between 2008 and 2020. The average renter aged 25-34 saw their deposit savings requirement increase by £32,000 over the same period. One generation accumulated wealth passively whilst sitting on assets. The other worked harder and fell further behind.

You're not competing in a meritocracy. You're competing in a wealth preservation system that was designed to protect the assets of people who bought property before the rules changed. And unless you inherited a deposit or can access the "Bank of Mum and Dad," the game was rigged before you sat down at the table.

The Information Gap That Determines Everything

Here's the part that changes the equation entirely: two buyers at identical income levels in the same city achieve completely different outcomes based purely on what they know.

Consider these two case studies from Birmingham, both earning £40,000 annually:

Buyer A - Timeline: 7 Years, Total Cost: £278,000

Sophie researched mortgages by Googling "best first-time buyer mortgage" and chose the product with the lowest headline rate: 3.2% over two years. She didn't understand LTV bands, so she saved for a 15% deposit thinking "more is better." She viewed properties based on Rightmove photos and emotional appeal. She bought a leasehold flat without reviewing the lease terms. The ground rent doubled every ten years, a clause buried on page 47 of the lease. She didn't commission a full structural survey to save £400. Six months after purchase, she discovered Japanese knotweed in the garden, costing £8,500 to remediate. Her mortgage deal expired, and she didn't remortgage in time, rolling onto the lender's standard variable rate (SVR) at 5.9%, costing an extra £178 monthly. Total excess costs from knowledge gaps: £47,000+.

Buyer B - Timeline: 18 Months, Total Cost: £231,000

James used a specialist first-time buyer mortgage broker who explained that 10% LTV products often have better rates than 15% LTV products due to lender risk appetite. He saved £24,000 instead of £36,000, reaching deposit readiness 14 months earlier. He attended viewings with a checklist covering structural red flags, leasehold terms, EPC ratings, and cladding compliance. He commissioned a Level 3 survey on his chosen property, which identified a roof issue. He renegotiated the purchase price down by £12,000 to cover repairs. He set a calendar reminder for his mortgage deal expiry and remortgaged six months in advance, securing a five-year fix at 3.4%. His broker explained overpayment flexibility, so he chose a product allowing 10% annual overpayments without penalty. Total savings from strategic knowledge: £47,000+.

Same city. Same income. Same market conditions. The only variable was information.

This is the hidden truth the UK property industry doesn't want you to understand: affordability isn't your problem, information asymmetry is. There are buyers earning £35,000 completing purchases in 18 months. There are buyers earning £55,000 still renting after eight years. The difference isn't money. It's knowledge.

The successful buyers know:

- Which government schemes help versus which ones trap you in poor-value properties
- How to structure deposits to maximise LTV efficiency rather than blindly "saving more"
- Which mortgage products offer genuine value over your likely ownership period, not just attractive headline rates

- How to identify property red flags that signal catastrophic costs: leasehold traps, structural defects, cladding issues, ground rent clauses
- When to negotiate, when to walk away, and when to accept based on comparable sales data
- How to time remortgages to avoid SVR penalties that silently drain thousands annually

This information isn't secret. It's just never presented as an integrated system. It's scattered across forums, hidden in broker jargon, buried in legal documents, and assumed as "common knowledge" by people who already own property.

You've spent hundreds of hours researching, and you feel less confident than when you started. That's not because you're incapable of learning. It's because you're trying to assemble a thousand scattered puzzle pieces without the picture on the box. The information environment is hostile by design, optimised to benefit people selling services, not people buying first homes.

Your Confusion Is Rational, Not Personal

Let me validate something you've been too afraid to admit: you feel stupid.

Not in your career. Not in your friendships. Not in any other area of your life. But when it comes to buying property, you feel like everyone else received an instruction manual that you somehow missed. You read articles about LTV ratios, freehold versus leasehold, mortgage arrangement fees, and early repayment charges, and your brain feels like it's moving through fog.

You wonder if you're just not smart enough for this. You wonder if successful buyers possess some innate financial intelligence you lack. You wonder if you're doomed to rent forever because you can't decode the complexity that seems obvious to everyone else.

Stop.

Your confusion isn't evidence of inadequacy. It's evidence of intelligence operating in a deliberately confusing environment.

The UK homebuying process is genuinely complex. It involves coordinating five specialist professionals (estate agents, mortgage brokers, solicitors, surveyors, and financial advisors), each speaking different technical languages and operating under different incentive structures. You're expected to make expert-level decisions on topics you've never encountered before: conveyancing timelines, building survey terminology, mortgage product structures, leasehold law, and property valuation methodology.

And you're expected to do this whilst working 45-55 hours per week in your actual job, with no formal training, no neutral advisor, and no ability to practice or fail safely. Imagine if your employer asked you to perform brain surgery based on Google research whilst maintaining your current workload. That's functionally what first-time buying demands.

The paralysis you feel when trying to compare mortgage products isn't personal failure. It's a rational response to genuine complexity. The anxiety you experience when viewing properties isn't evidence of inadequacy. It's appropriate caution when making a £250,000 decision with irreversible consequences.

Your struggle is structural, not personal. The system is designed to be confusing because confusion benefits the people selling services. Confused buyers accept higher fees, miss better deals, and don't ask challenging questions. Confident buyers shop around, negotiate, and reduce profit margins.

The industry doesn't want you to feel confident. It wants you to feel grateful that someone, anyone, is willing to "help" you achieve homeownership. That gratitude translates into higher commissions, larger fees, and less scrutiny of the advice you're receiving.

The £40,000 Cost of Not Knowing

Let me quantify exactly what knowledge gaps cost in real terms.

According to research by the Homeowners Alliance and MoneySavingExpert, the average first-time buyer makes five catastrophic mistakes that could have been avoided with strategic information:

1. **Wrong mortgage product selection**: Choosing based on headline rate instead of total cost over likely ownership period. Average excess cost: £8,200

2. **Unsuitable property purchase**: Buying leasehold with punitive terms, or freehold with structural defects missed during viewing. Average excess cost: £12,000

3. **Inefficient deposit strategy**: Saving more than required or using wrong savings vehicles. Average timeline extension: 14 months (opportunity cost: £9,800 in rent)

4. **Missed scheme opportunities**: Not maximising Lifetime ISA, Help to Buy ISA, or shared ownership where appropriate. Average excess cost: £4,100

5. **Poor remortgage timing**: Rolling onto SVR or not shopping around at deal expiry. Average excess cost: £6,400 over five years

Total average cost of knowledge gaps: £40,500.

But the real cost isn't just financial, it's temporal. Those 14 months of extended timeline translate into 14 months of continued rent payments, 14 months of property price appreciation widening the deposit gap, and 14 months of psychological weight knowing you're no closer to ownership.

Knowledge gaps don't just cost money. They steal time you'll never recover. They delay family planning. They postpone career moves. They extend the period where you feel like a failed adult in your mid-thirties whilst peers with parental help buy their second properties.

The brutal economics are simple: learning what you need to know is worth £40,000 and 3-5 years of your life. That's not an exaggeration. That's the measured cost of ignorance in the UK property market.

You've just confronted the hardest truth of your homebuying journey: the system is designed against you. But here's the revelation that makes this chapter the foundation of everything that follows: the variable you can control is knowledge, not affordability.

You can't change house price appreciation. You can't reverse quantitative easing. You can't access parental wealth you don't have. But you can acquire the strategic information that separates successful first-time buyers from perpetual renters, and that knowledge converts your current income into homeownership.

The next chapter reveals the true cost of continuing down the path you're on guesswork. Every decision you make without precise financial truth and strategic knowledge is a gamble with stakes you can't afford to lose. We're going to establish exactly what guesswork costs, and why the paralysis-by-research pattern you're trapped in is actively destroying your confidence instead of building it.

The game was rigged. But you're about to learn how to play it anyway.

The True Cost of Guesswork

Sarah spent 140 hours researching mortgages and felt more confused than when she started.

She'd bookmarked 47 articles, watched 23 YouTube videos, and joined four Facebook groups for first-time buyers. Her spreadsheet had 18 tabs comparing mortgage products. Her browser history was a graveyard of abandoned research sessions at 2am. Yet when her estate agent asked what she could afford, she froze. She'd consumed information for six months straight and couldn't answer the most basic question about her own homebuying journey. Sarah isn't unusual, she's typical. And her confusion isn't personal failure.

It's the predictable cost of operating on guesswork instead of knowledge.

The UK property market doesn't reward hard work or good intentions. It rewards precision. And the gap between researching endlessly and knowing exactly what to do is costing first time buyers like you between £30,000 and £50,000 in mistakes you can't see coming. This chapter reveals why.

The Maths That Generic Advice Can't Solve

"Just save more" is the most common advice given to aspiring first-time buyers. It's also mathematically useless.

Here's why: without knowing your exact income, monthly outgoings, target property price, required deposit percentage, and current savings rate, the instruction to "save more" provides zero actionable guidance. It's the equivalent of telling someone lost in London to "walk faster" without giving them a destination or map.

Let me show you the actual maths. Take two buyers, both 32 years old, both earning £45,000 annually in Manchester, both aiming to buy a £200,000 property requiring a £20,000 deposit (10% LTV). On paper, they're identical.

Buyer A follows generic advice. She knows she needs to "save more" and commits to being "disciplined." She transfers £400 per month into a standard savings account earning 0.5% interest. She researches mortgage options sporadically but hasn't calculated her exact borrowing capacity. She vaguely knows about Lifetime ISAs but hasn't investigated eligibility. She's "doing her best."

Buyer B establishes precise baseline data in Week 1. She calculates that at £45,000 salary, her maximum borrowing is approximately £202,500 (4.5x income multiplier). She needs exactly £20,000 deposit plus £3,000 for fees and moving costs, total £23,000. She currently has £8,000 saved. She needs £15,000 more. She opens a Lifetime ISA immediately, receiving a 25% government bonus on contributions up to £4,000 annually. She automates £500 monthly transfers on payday. Her precision reveals she'll be deposit-ready in 27 months, not "someday."

Same income. Same target property. Radically different timelines.

Buyer A reaches £20,000 in saved capital after 48 months, four years of disciplined saving. She's lost £4,000 in potential government bonuses by not using a Lifetime ISA. She's lost approximately £800 in higher interest rates available through fixed-term savings accounts. Total opportunity cost: £4,800. Timeline: 48 months.

Buyer B reaches £23,000 in total capital after 27 months, less than half Buyer A's timeline. She's gained £2,000 in government bonuses. She's optimised interest returns. Timeline: 27 months.

The timeline difference: 21 months. The financial difference: £4,800.

And this is before either buyer has made an offer on a property. This is purely the accumulation phase. The "just save more" advice cost Buyer A nearly two years and £5,000 because it lacked precision. She worked just as hard. She was just as disciplined. But guesswork extended her timeline by 44%.

Now multiply this across every decision in the homebuying journey, mortgage product selection, property evaluation, offer strategy, survey response, and you start to see why unprepared buyers consistently lose £30,000-£50,000+ compared to those operating with structured knowledge.

Generic advice isn't harmless. It's expensive.

The Catastrophic Mistakes You Can't See Yet

Let me introduce you to three real buyers who made decisions that seemed perfectly reasonable at the time. Each mistake cost them between £28,000 and £53,000. None of them realised the error until it was too late.

Case Study 1: Tom, The Mortgage Product Trap

Tom, 34, bought a £285,000 flat in Bristol in 2019. He compared mortgage rates obsessively and chose the absolute lowest rate available: 1.49% fixed for two years. The arrangement fee was £1,999, which he added to the mortgage. He felt brilliant, he'd beaten the system by securing the best rate on the market.

What Tom didn't calculate: the true cost over his likely ownership period.

The product had a 5% early repayment charge (ERC) for the entire two-year fixed period. When Tom's circumstances changed 18 months later, his partner got a job offer in Edinburgh, he wanted to sell. The ERC was £14,250. He couldn't afford to pay it, so he stayed in Bristol, commuting to Edinburgh twice monthly at £180 per trip. Over 12 months, he spent £4,320 on train fares and lost the Edinburgh job opportunity worth an additional £8,000 annually in salary progression.

Then his two-year fixed rate ended in March 2021. He moved to the lender's standard variable rate at 4.2% while researching remortgage options, adding £347 monthly to his mortgage payments. He delayed for four months (indecision paralysis from his last mortgage experience), costing £1,388.

Total financial damage from selecting the "best rate" without understanding product structure:

- Lost job opportunity over two years: £16,000
- Unnecessary commuting costs: £4,320
- SVR overpayment during indecision: £1,388
- **Total: £21,708**

Tom chose the lowest rate. He lost £21,708 because he didn't understand that mortgage products are systems, not just interest rates. The headline rate was brilliant. The product structure was a trap.

Case Study 2: Emma, The Leasehold Nightmare

Emma, 29, bought a £190,000 leasehold flat in Reading in 2018. The ground rent was £250 annually, seemed reasonable. The lease had 95 years remaining, well above the 80-year threshold she'd read about online. She felt confident she'd done her research.

What Emma didn't investigate: the ground rent escalation clause buried on page 47 of the lease.

The ground rent doubled every 10 years. Year 1-10: £250. Year 11-20: £500. Year 21-30: £1,000. Year 31-40: £2,000. By year 50, it would be £8,000 annually. The lease was toxic.

When Emma tried to sell in 2023 after five years of ownership, three mortgage lenders rejected her buyer's applications outright, they'd blacklisted leases with doubling ground rent clauses post-2017 regulation changes. She eventually found a cash buyer, but had to accept £167,000, £23,000 below market value for equivalent freeholds in her area.

She'd also paid £1,250 in ground rent over five years, plus £180 annually in service charges that increased 6% yearly without justification, totalling £1,014.

Total financial damage from not scrutinising the lease structure:

- Forced sale below market value: £23,000
- Ground rent paid: £1,250
- Service charge overpayment: £1,014
- **Total: £25,264**

Emma researched lease length. She missed ground rent escalation. That single oversight cost her £25,264.

Case Study 3: James, The Survey Gamble

James, 36, bought a £310,000 Victorian terrace in Liverpool in 2020. He commissioned a Homebuyers Report (mid-tier survey) at £580 rather than a full structural survey at £850 to save money. The Homebuyers Report noted "some minor cracking to the rear elevation, monitor but not alarming."

Eighteen months later, the rear wall needed underpinning. Cost: £32,000.

James's buildings insurance refused the claim, the surveyor's report had noted cracking, which meant it was a "pre-existing condition" rather than sudden damage. He took out a high-interest loan at 9.8% APR to cover the emergency repair, paying £38,150 total over five years.

Had he commissioned a structural survey for £850, the underpinning requirement would have been identified pre-purchase. He could have renegotiated the purchase price down by £30,000, walked away, or required the seller to complete repairs before exchange.

Total financial damage from choosing the cheaper survey:

- Underpinning cost: £32,000
- Loan interest over five years: £6,150
- **Total: £38,150**

Minus the £850 structural survey he didn't commission, James's "saving" of £270 (difference between Homebuyers Report and full survey) cost him £37,300 in actual financial damage.

Three buyers. Three decisions that seemed sensible. Combined losses: £84,172.

None of these mistakes announced themselves. Tom didn't know mortgage ERCs could trap him geographically. Emma didn't know ground rent clauses could make properties unsellable. James didn't know Homebuyers Reports aren't structural surveys. They were operating on guesswork, not knowledge. And guesswork in the UK property market is catastrophically expensive.

When More Research Makes Everything Worse

Here's the paradox that first time buyers find most destabilising: the more you research, the less confident you feel.

You'd expect the opposite. You're intelligent. You're analytically minded. Surely 100 hours of research should produce more confidence than 10 hours. But it doesn't. Instead, you're trapped in a cycle where every new article contradicts the previous one, every forum thread introduces a new variable you hadn't considered, and every "expert opinion" conflicts with the last.

This isn't personal weakness. It's predictable human psychology when consuming unstructured information without decision frameworks.

You're living this paradox. You've consumed MoneySavingExpert forums, Which? guides, broker comparison sites, YouTube explainers, and government scheme documentation. You know the difference between fixed and variable rates, understand LTV bands, and can explain stamp duty thresholds. You're objectively information rich.

But when it's time to make an actual decision, should I fix for two years or five? Is this property worth £15,000 over asking? Should I use a broker or go direct?, you freeze.

Because you can construct equally compelling arguments for contradictory actions using the information you've consumed.

This is the difference between information and knowledge. Information is facts without framework. Knowledge is structured understanding that enables confident action.

Let me show you what this looks like in practice. You're researching whether to use a mortgage broker or apply directly to lenders. You read:

- Article A: "Brokers have access to exclusive products you can't get direct, essential for first-time buyers."
- Article B: "Broker fees of £500-£1,000 are unnecessary, you can research products yourself for free."
- Forum Post C: "My broker saved me £200 monthly, worth every penny of the £995 fee."
- Forum Post D: "I went direct and got the same rate the broker quoted, saved myself £500."

You now have four data points. Zero clarity. Because you don't have the framework to evaluate WHEN brokers add value versus when they don't. The information is contradictory because it's context-dependent, but you don't have the decision tree that reveals which context you're in.

A knowledge-equipped buyer knows brokers add maximum value when your income is complex (self-employed, contractor, multiple jobs), when you have credit history complications, or when you're time-poor and value consolidated search. They add minimal value when you have straightforward PAYE income, clean credit, and enjoy research.

Same information. Different outcome. One buyer stays researching for another month. The other makes a confident decision in 20 minutes.

Your paralysis-by-research isn't evidence that you need to read more. It's evidence that you need the organizing framework that converts information into knowledge. And that's what the RENTER Framework delivers.

Information-Rich but Knowledge-Starved

You already possess sufficient information to buy your first home successfully. What you're missing is the structure to deploy it.

This distinction, information versus knowledge, is the single most important concept in this entire book. Get this right, and your paralysis ends. Miss this, and you'll still be researching in three years.

Information is raw facts: mortgage rates, house prices, deposit requirements, scheme eligibility criteria. You can acquire information through Google searches, forum scrolling, and article reading. It's abundant. It's free. And first time buyers have consumed more property-buying information than any previous generation.

Knowledge is structured frameworks for decision-making: the precise sequence of steps, the go/no-go criteria at each decision node, the context-dependent rules that tell you which information actually matters for YOUR specific situation.

You're information rich. You know what a Lifetime ISA is, how LTV ratios work, and why credit scores matter. But you're knowledge starved. You don't know whether YOU should use a Lifetime ISA given your timeline and target location. You don't know which LTV band to target given your income and relationship status. You don't know how to improve your credit score in the specific ways that mortgage lenders actually care about.

The information exists in your browser history. The knowledge exists in structured systems. This book delivers the system.

Your Financial Picture Is Wrong, In Both Directions

Here's what happens when first-time buyers finally conduct a complete financial audit: they discover they've been systematically wrong about their financial position in two opposite directions simultaneously.

They've overestimated barriers that don't actually exist. And they've underestimated assets they already possess.

Overestimated Barriers:

You probably believe your credit score is worse than it is. Most first time buyers do. You missed a mobile phone payment three years ago, you have student loans, you've switched current accounts twice, surely your credit is damaged?

Actual data: 73% of first-time buyers who completed baseline credit checks discovered their score was 50-150 points higher than they estimated. Student loans don't negatively impact credit scores, they're simply factored into affordability calculations. And the missed phone payment from 2021? It's already aged off your Experian report.

You probably believe you need a larger deposit than you actually do. The cultural narrative says "20% deposit minimum" but actual lending practice in 2024 shows 64% of first-time buyers in England purchased with 5-10% deposits using government schemes and guarantor options.

You probably believe your income is too low. But buyers at your exact salary level are completing purchases every month in your target city. They're not earning more; they're operating with better information.

Underestimated Assets:

You probably haven't calculated your true borrowing capacity. Quick exercise: multiply your annual salary by 4.5. That's your approximate maximum mortgage as a solo buyer. Couple? Combine salaries and multiply by 4.5. Most readers just discovered they can borrow £20,000-£40,000 more than they thought.

You probably haven't checked Lifetime ISA eligibility. If you're under 40 and buying a property under £450,000, you're receiving a 25% government bonus on £4,000 annual contributions, free money you're currently leaving on the table.

You probably have savings deployed inefficiently. Money sitting in current accounts earning 0.1% interest when it could be in fixed-term accounts earning 4-5%. Over 18 months, that's £600-£800 in lost returns on a £15,000 deposit fund.

When you establish financial precision through the Reveal stage of the RENTER Framework, both distortions correct simultaneously. Barriers you thought were blocking you disappear. Assets you didn't know you had appear. And your timeline often compresses by 12-18 months purely through accurate information.

Sarah from the chapter opening? She finally stopped researching and started executing. She completed a full financial audit, discovered she was 14 months closer to deposit-ready than she'd believed, and had enough borrowing capacity to target properties £25,000 higher in value than she thought possible.

The guesswork had cost her 18 months of paralysis. The precision gave her back control.

You now understand why guesswork is catastrophically expensive and why your perpetual research loop isn't building confidence, it's destroying it. The next chapter reveals what actually separates successful buyers from perpetual renters at your exact income level, and why the differentiator has never been affordability. It's always been knowledge.

Turn the page, and you'll discover which of the four Millennial Buyer Matrix profiles you belong to, and the precise pathway designed for your situation.

What Actually Separates Buyers from Renters

The UK housing market hasn't locked you out because of your salary.

The brutal truth is simpler and far more solvable: you've been competing in an information war you didn't know you'd entered, armed with generic advice designed for someone else's circumstances while your peers who succeeded understood the specific playbook for buyers exactly like them. The difference between homeowners at your income level and perpetual renters isn't money, it's knowledge, applied systematically at six critical moments that determine whether you complete in 18 months or remain paralysed for years. This chapter rewrites the narrative you've been sold about why you're "not ready yet" and replaces it with the framework that explains why successful buyers without family wealth exist at every income bracket, in every UK city, navigating the same impossible-looking mathematics you're facing right now.

The Three Categories That Define Every First-Time Buyer's Journey

Every first-time buyer in the UK falls into one of three distinct categories, and understanding which one you occupy changes everything about your strategy and timeline.

Category One: The Subsidised Buyers. These are the buyers property journalists love profiling, 28-year-old marketing coordinators holding keys to two-bedroom flats in Clapham, crediting their "savings discipline" in interviews whilst carefully omitting the £60,000 deposit gift from parents. They represent roughly 40% of first-time buyers under 35 in London and the South East, and approximately 25% in regional cities. Their homeownership is real, but their pathway is fundamentally inaccessible to you. The cognitive dissonance comes from watching someone at your exact income level succeed whilst you struggle, not recognising that you're playing entirely different games. They weren't better savers. They had subsidised entry.

Category Two: The Knowledge-Equipped Buyers. This is the category you're about to join. These buyers earn £30,000-£60,000, carry student debt, receive zero family financial support, and own homes anyway. They represent roughly 35% of first-time buyer completions, a significant minority that mainstream narratives ignore because their success disrupts the fatalistic "Generation Rent" storyline. What separates them isn't exceptional circumstances or lottery-win salaries. It's structured information applied at specific decision points: which government scheme genuinely accelerates their timeline versus which one traps them, how to position their credit profile to access top-quartile mortgage rates, which property types in which neighbourhoods represent genuine value versus marketing illusions, and when to walk away from deals that look acceptable but contain catastrophic long-term costs. They compressed timelines from 6-8 years to 18-24 months not through deprivation, but through intelligent architecture.

Category Three: The Perpetually Paralysed. These are the buyers who never complete. Not because they lack income, discipline, or desire, but because they're trapped in the paradox of information overwhelm creating decision paralysis. They've read everything, researched obsessively, attended first-time buyer seminars, spoken to three mortgage brokers, and feel less confident than when they started. They represent roughly 25% of serious first-time buyer aspirants who remain renters indefinitely despite having sufficient income to succeed. Their tragedy isn't financial, it's informational. They're drowning in data whilst starving for knowledge, unable to distinguish signal from noise, and interpreting their confusion as evidence of personal inadequacy rather than recognising it as the predictable outcome of consuming generic advice designed for someone else's matrix position.

You've likely spent years believing you're in Category Three, destined to remain there until some external variable changes, a promotion, an inheritance, a market crash. This chapter proves you're actually in Category Two already. You simply haven't been given the operating system yet.

Why "Affordability" Is the Wrong Lens Entirely

The most damaging lie the UK property market tells is that homeownership is purely a function of affordability, that your inability to buy is simple mathematics: house prices too high, your salary too low, equation unsolvable. This framing is convenient for policymakers, journalists, and the industry itself because it positions the problem as structural and therefore unsolvable at the individual level. It's also provably false.

The Evidence from Your Income Bracket

Let's examine the 2023 UK Finance data on first-time buyer completions by income band:

Annual Income	Median Purchase Price	Typical Deposit	London/SE FTB %	Regional FTB %
£30,000-£35,000	£168,000	£16,800	12%	31%
£35,000-£45,000	£195,000	£19,500	18%	38%
£45,000-£60,000	£242,000	£24,200	27%	42%

These aren't outliers. These are median completions, meaning half of buyers in each income band purchased below these prices, half above. If homeownership were purely about affordability, these completions wouldn't exist. Someone earning £32,000 in Manchester cannot "afford" a £170,000 property any more than someone earning £32,000 in Manchester who remains a renter can. The difference isn't affordability. It's information.

The Two Variables That Actually Matter

Successful buyers without family help understand that homeownership isn't determined by a single affordability calculation, it's determined by two variables working in combination:

1. **Deposit velocity:** How quickly you accumulate the required 10-15% deposit through intelligent financial architecture, scheme optimisation, and expense restructuring

2. **Borrowing maximisation:** How effectively you position yourself to access the highest lending multiple your income allows, at the most competitive rates available

A buyer earning £38,000 who understands these variables, implementing a Lifetime ISA correctly, restructuring their credit profile six months before mortgage application, and eliminating silent financial drag, can complete 18-24 months faster than an identical buyer earning £42,000 who doesn't. The higher earner's income advantage gets neutralised by their information disadvantage. This isn't theoretical. You're about to see it proven in forensic detail.

The Millennial Buyer Matrix: Your Personalised Pathway

Generic first-time buyer advice fails because it treats all buyers as a homogeneous group when the reality is that your pathway depends entirely on three variables: income level, geographic location, and relationship status. These create four distinct matrix positions, each requiring fundamentally different strategies.

Matrix Position	Income Profile	Deposit Timeline	Property Type Focus	Primary Challenge
Solo, Regional	£30k-£45k	18-24 months	2-bed terraces, flats	Maximising single-income borrowing
Couple, Regional	£60k-£90k combined	12-18 months	2-3 bed houses	Decision coordination, contribution fairness
Solo, London/SE	£40k-£60k	24-36 months	1-bed flats, Shared Ownership	Extreme price-to-income ratios
Couple, London/SE	£80k-£120k combined	18-24 months	2-bed flats, commuter houses	Balancing location vs affordability

Understanding your matrix position immediately explains why certain advice you've received felt useless. A solo buyer in Birmingham reading guidance written for couples in London will experience every recommendation as irrelevant or impossible. The deposit timelines don't match. The property types don't exist in their market. The strategic priorities are inverted.

Your Matrix Position Determines Everything

If you're a **solo regional buyer** earning £38,000 in Leeds, your primary strategic focus is maximising your borrowing multiple through credit positioning and potentially accessing the 5.5x income lending products available to well-positioned applicants. Your deposit timeline is 18-24 months with a £15,000-£20,000 target. Your property search focuses on two-bedroom terraced houses in areas with strong transport connectivity.

If you're a **couple in London** with combined income of £85,000, your challenge isn't borrowing capacity, it's deposit accumulation in a market requiring £35,000-£45,000 minimum. Your strategic focus is deposit velocity through dual Lifetime ISA maximisation and aggressive expense optimisation. Your property search likely involves geographic radius expansion or Shared Ownership evaluation.

The framework you're about to implement adapts to your matrix position. The six decision nodes remain constant. The specific strategies at each node vary by position.

The Six Decision Nodes Where Knowledge Separates Outcomes

There are six moments in every homebuying journey where lack of specific information causes either irreversible timeline damage or catastrophic financial loss. These aren't continuous states, they're discrete decision points where you choose a path, and that choice creates consequences that compound for years.

Node One: Government Scheme Selection (Month 1-2)

The decision: Lifetime ISA (LISA), Shared Ownership, or none. An uninformed buyer often chooses based on marketing appeal or friend recommendation. A knowledge-equipped buyer evaluates against their matrix position and timeline. Wrong choice here can trap you in unsuitable property types (Shared Ownership) or cost you £8,000-£12,000 in lost bonus growth (choosing no scheme when LISA would have accelerated timeline).

Node Two: Credit Profile Positioning (Month 3-6)

The decision: When and how to address credit file errors, optimise credit utilisation, and structure existing debt. Uninformed buyers discover credit issues during mortgage application, too late to fix. Knowledge-equipped buyers audit and optimise six months before they need their Agreement in Principle, converting themselves from "declined" or "standard rate" to "top quartile approved." This single node determines whether you access 4.5% rates or 5.8% rates, a difference costing £3,600 on a £200,000 mortgage over two years.

Node Three: Mortgage Product Selection (Month 12-14)

The decision: Which of 3,000+ products matches your risk profile, ownership timeline, and circumstances. Uninformed buyers choose based on headline rate alone. Knowledge-equipped buyers evaluate true cost over likely ownership period, factoring in arrangement fees, early repayment charges, overpayment flexibility, and portability. Wrong choice costs £5,000-£15,000 in unnecessary fees or trapped equity.

Node Four: Property Evaluation (Month 14-16)

The decision: Which properties represent genuine value versus which are money pits disguised as bargains. Uninformed buyers fall in love with aesthetics and ignore structural red flags, leasehold traps, or area fundamentals. Knowledge-equipped buyers apply the Property Intelligence Filter, walking away from 80% of viewings and making offers only on the 20% that pass all criteria. Wrong choice here can cost £30,000-£50,000+ in repair costs, service charge increases, or negative equity.

Node Five: Offer Strategy and Negotiation (Month 16-17)

The decision: Opening offer calculation, leveraging first-time buyer status, and knowing when to walk. Uninformed buyers either overpay through fear of losing the property or under-offer and alienate sellers. Knowledge-equipped buyers use comparable evidence and seller motivation analysis to make competitive offers that win without overpaying. Wrong approach costs £8,000-£15,000 in overpayment or months in failed negotiations.

Node Six: Survey Response and Deal Protection (Month 17-18)

The decision: How to interpret survey findings, when to renegotiate, when to walk away. Uninformed buyers panic at minor issues or ignore catastrophic ones. Knowledge-equipped buyers use go/no-go criteria, protecting themselves from completing on unsuitable properties whilst avoiding deal-breaking over cosmetic concerns. Wrong decision either traps you in a property requiring £20,000+ unexpected work or causes you to walk from a sound purchase over repairable issues.

These six nodes are where your journey gets won or lost. The rest of the process is administration. These are the moments where information becomes financially measurable advantage.

The Tale of Two Buyers: Lisa and Matthew

Let me show you what information asymmetry looks like in practice. Lisa and Matthew both earn £38,000 annually working in marketing roles in Birmingham. Both are 31 years old, both single, both without family financial support, both starting their homebuying journey in January 2022. Three and a half years later, Lisa has owned her two-bedroom terrace in Moseley for 20 months. Matthew remains a renter, convinced he "cannot afford to buy yet."

Lisa's Knowledge-Equipped Journey

Lisa spent her first weekend conducting a complete financial audit using the Reveal stage framework. She discovered she had £6,200 in accessible savings, was losing £140 monthly to optimisable subscriptions and inefficient accounts, and her credit file showed an error from a closed mobile contract incorrectly marked as defaulted. She opened a Lifetime ISA in February 2022, automated £280 monthly deposits, and disputed the credit file error, resolved by April 2022.

By July 2022, Lisa had implemented the deposit velocity system, restructured her expenses without life sacrifice, and projected deposit readiness for January 2023. She secured her Agreement in Principle in November 2022, top quartile approval at 4.4% with 4.5x income lending, £171,000 maximum. She began active property searching in December 2022 with precision parameters: two-bedroom terraced houses, Moseley/Balsall Heath/Kings Heath, £160,000-£175,000 range, freehold only.

Lisa viewed 12 properties over eight weeks, applied the Property Intelligence Filter at each viewing, and walked away from 11. The 12th, a two-bedroom terrace in Moseley listed at £169,950, passed all criteria. She offered £162,000 using comparable evidence, seller accepted at £164,500. Survey revealed minor roof repairs needed; she renegotiated to £163,000. Completed July 2023, 18 months after beginning her journey.

Matthew's Information-Poor Journey

Matthew spent his first six months "researching" by reading generic articles, watching YouTube videos, and joining first-time buyer Facebook groups. He didn't open a Lifetime ISA because he "wasn't sure if it was the right choice yet." He didn't audit his credit file. He saved sporadically into an easy-access account earning 0.1% interest, averaging £180 monthly when he remembered.

By July 2022, Matthew had £4,800 saved, £2,000 less than Lisa despite identical income, because he lacked automated architecture. He finally applied for a Lifetime ISA in August 2022, realising he'd lost six months of bonus growth. He didn't secure an Agreement in Principle because he "wasn't ready to commit to searching yet."

Matthew began casually browsing Rightmove in March 2023, viewing properties without clear search parameters or evaluation framework. He fell in love with a two-bedroom flat in Digbeth listed at £185,000, above his realistic budget but "such good value." He made an offer without an AIP, which was rejected. When he finally secured an AIP in June 2023, he discovered the credit file error Lisa had found 14 months earlier, his approval was limited to £155,000 at 5.9%.

Matthew remains paralysed in March 2026, having viewed 30+ properties over three years without making a successful offer. His Lifetime ISA now holds £14,200. He believes he needs "another year or two of saving" when the reality is he needed structured knowledge three years ago.

The 18-Month Timeline Difference

Lisa and Matthew faced identical market conditions, identical income, identical starting points. The only variable was information. Lisa completed in 18 months because she understood the six decision nodes and executed correctly at each. Matthew remains a renter after 38 months because he's navigating blindly, making predictable mistakes at every node, interpreting his struggle as evidence the system is unbeatable rather than recognising it as the natural consequence of applying generic information to his specific matrix position.

You are Lisa's income twin in your city. The question isn't whether you can afford to buy. The question is whether you're ready to stop being Matthew.

The revelation that knowledge, not income, determines your timeline should feel simultaneously validating and activating. Validating because your struggle was never evidence of personal failure. Activating because you now understand the specific variable you can control. The next chapter introduces you to the complete system that converts this understanding into irreversible forward momentum: the Renter Liberation System and its six-stage RENTER Framework, your personalised operating system for the 18-month journey from paralysed renter to proud homeowner.

Your Liberation System

Everything you've been told about buying your first home is backwards.

The traditional advice, save more, wait longer, hope harder, treats homeownership as a waiting game you'll eventually win through sheer persistence. But here's what that advice deliberately ignores: without the right system, you're not waiting to win. You're waiting to fail more expensively. The difference between buyers who complete in 18 months and renters who remain paralysed for 6-8 years isn't income, luck, or market timing. It's knowledge structured into a system that works.

This chapter introduces the Renter Liberation System; the only framework built specifically for first time buyers buying without parental help in today's UK market. You'll understand why it works when generic advice fails, how it compresses timelines without requiring life sacrifice, and what commitment it demands from you.

The System Traditional Resources Won't Give You

Walk into any high-street estate agent or browse the government's first-time buyer resources, and you'll find the same recycled guidance: open a Lifetime ISA, check your credit score, get a mortgage in principle, start viewing properties. These aren't wrong steps, they're just catastrophically incomplete. It's like being handed a recipe that lists ingredients but skips the cooking instructions, serving temperatures, and the warning that substituting salt for sugar will poison everyone at the table.

Here's the structural problem with every mainstream first-time buyer resource: they optimize for completion, not sustainable ownership. Their success metric is "keys in hand." Yours should be "solvent homeowner 12 months later." That gap, between completion and genuine stability, is where unprepared buyers financially drown.

Consider Mandy, a 31-year-old marketing manager in Manchester earning £38,000. She followed traditional advice perfectly: saved her deposit over five years, secured a mortgage, bought a two-bedroom flat in a regeneration area, completed in March 2022. By December 2022, she was in crisis. Her boiler failed (£2,800), the building needed emergency cladding remediation (£6,000 service charge), and her fixed-rate mortgage was ending just as rates spiked. She had no emergency fund; she'd depleted everything to maximize her deposit. Traditional advice got her to completion. It didn't prepare her for ownership.

Now consider Alan and Rebecca, a couple in Birmingham, combined income £52,000. They used the Renter Liberation System. They completed in October 2022 with a smaller deposit but a fully funded six-month emergency reserve. When their boiler failed in January 2023, they paid cash. When their mortgage deal ended, they'd overpaid enough to reduce their LTV and secure a better rate. Same market conditions as Mandy. Opposite financial outcomes. The difference wasn't income, it was system.

Traditional resources fail because they're designed for a different buyer. They assume parental safety nets to absorb mistakes. They assume weekday flexibility for viewings and solicitor calls. They assume financial literacy you were never taught. They assume margin for error you don't possess. The Renter Liberation System assumes none of this. It's built for buyers who work 50-hour weeks, carry student debt, manage tight budgets, and need every decision protected because there's no family bailout waiting.

The RENTER Framework: Your Identity Becomes Your Process

The word at the heart of this system is the identity you're trying to escape. **RENTER** isn't just a label, it's your six-stage roadmap from paralysis to keys in hand to genuinely stable ownership. Each letter represents a sequential stage that builds irreversible forward momentum toward the next.

Here's the complete framework:

R, Reveal: Uncover your true financial starting point through complete transparency. No guesswork, no optimistic assumptions, no distorted self-perception. You'll conduct a full financial audit covering income, outgoings, existing savings, student loans, and credit profile across all three UK agencies. You'll use the Deposit Velocity Calculator to determine your precise monthly savings requirement and projected deposit readiness date. You'll identify which of the four Millennial Buyer Matrix profiles matches your situation, solo outside London, couple outside London, solo in London/SE, couple in

London/SE. This stage converts "someday I'll own a home" into "deposit ready by Month X, Year Y."

E, Engineer: Build your 18-month financial runway through intelligent architecture, not deprivation. You'll evaluate government schemes using the honest assessment matrix that shows when Lifetime ISAs help versus trap. You'll implement the Deposit Velocity System by restructuring expenses into non-negotiable, optimisable, and eliminable tiers. You'll automate monthly savings transfers on payday so accumulation requires zero willpower. You'll stress-test your runway to ensure you reach exchange with a 3-6 month emergency fund intact, not depleted. This stage compresses timelines from 6-8 years to 18 months without monastic sacrifice.

N, Navigate: Master mortgages and maximize borrowing power before you make a single offer. You'll execute the three-stage Mortgage Confidence Blueprint: audit your current capacity, implement the six specific improvements that increase your Agreement in Principle, and secure your AIP at least 60 days before active searching. You'll use the Mortgage Product Shortlist Filter to narrow 3,000+ products to the three best-suited candidates for your exact circumstances. You'll understand true cost over your likely ownership period, not just headline rate. This stage converts mortgage confusion into strategic advantage.

T, Target: Identify, evaluate, and select the right property using the Property Intelligence Filter. You'll assess structural integrity, leasehold risks, EPC compliance, post-Grenfell cladding safety, area fundamentals, and investment merit within a single viewing. You'll use the Neighbourhood Fundamentals Scorecard to evaluate transport connectivity, regeneration pipelines, school trajectories, and landlord-to-owner ratios. You'll set precision search parameters on Rightmove and Zoopla matched to your Matrix profile. This stage transforms you from anxious viewer into strategic evaluator who never confuses a money pit for a bargain.

E, Execute: Make your offer, protect the deal, and complete without catastrophic errors. You'll use the Offer Intelligence Protocol to assess seller motivation and comparable evidence before calculating your opening bid. You'll apply the Guardian Framework's ten catastrophic mistake checkpoints at every decision node, survey response, mortgage selection, contract exchange, completion. You'll implement the Deal Protection Checklist to manage solicitors, surveyors, and brokers in parallel using the 5-Hour Weekend Method. This stage guides you through the active purchase phase with confidence and protection.

R, Reside: Transition successfully into proud, solvent homeownership through the critical first 12 months. You'll execute the Post-Purchase Financial Reset Plan within 30 days, recalibrating your budget for mortgage payments, council tax, insurance, and maintenance reserves. You'll use the Emergency Fund Rebuild Protocol to restore your three-month buffer within six months. You'll complete the Homeowner Identity Consolidation checklist, utilities, Land Registry, insurance setup, maintenance calendar. This stage ensures you arrive not just as a homeowner, but as a financially resilient one.

Each stage builds on the last. You can't Engineer an effective deposit runway without Revealing your true baseline. You can't Navigate mortgages effectively without knowing your engineered savings capacity. You can't Target properties strategically without understanding your mortgage approval limits. You can't Execute confidently without having targeted the right property type. And you can't Reside successfully without having protected yourself throughout Execution.

The framework is sequential by design. Skipping stages or shuffling the order destroys the compounding effect. This isn't a menu of tips you can cherry-pick. It's an operating system you implement completely.

How 18 Months Becomes Possible Without Life Sacrifice

The dominant narrative says faster timelines require extreme sacrifice: move back with parents, eliminate all discretionary spending, work three jobs, abandon social life, defer relationships. That's not compression, that's life suspension. And for most first time buyers, it's neither possible nor desirable.

The Renter Liberation System compresses timelines through intelligent architecture, not monastic deprivation. Here's how:

Automation eliminates willpower dependency. Instead of manually transferring savings each month, where a difficult week becomes an excuse to skip, you set up automatic payday transfers into a separate savings account. The decision happens once. The execution happens forever. This single structural change prevents the monthly willpower battle that quietly extends timelines by 12-18 months.

Strategic expense restructuring identifies hidden financial drag. Most renters unknowingly carry £150-£300 monthly in optimisable or eliminable spending: subscriptions they forgot existed, inefficient mobile contracts, retail banking fees, duplicate insurance policies. The Deposit Velocity System categorizes every expense as non-negotiable (rent, utilities, student loans), optimisable (insurance, phone contracts, gym memberships), or eliminable (unused subscriptions, convenience spending). Restructuring optimisable expenses alone typically frees £100-£200 monthly without lifestyle sacrifice.

Government scheme optimization captures free money. A 25% government bonus on Lifetime ISA contributions up to £4,000 annually represents £1,000 of free deposit acceleration. But the scheme has traps, withdrawal penalties, property price caps, first-home restrictions. The honest scheme assessment shows exactly when LISAs help versus trap based on your Matrix profile, ensuring you capture benefits without triggering penalties.

Protection-first decision-making prevents catastrophic timeline resets. A single major mistake, buying a property with undisclosed structural issues, selecting a mortgage with punitive early repayment charges, failing to budget for post-purchase cash flow, can extend your timeline by 2-5 years through forced sales, refinancing costs, or emergency debt. The Guardian Framework's go/no-go checkpoints prevent these catastrophic errors, protecting your timeline more effectively than marginal optimization ever could.

Here's a worked example. Emma, 29, solo buyer in Leeds, earning £36,000:

- **Traditional timeline**: Save £200 monthly → 7.5 years to reach £18,000 deposit (5% of £360,000 target property after accounting for London/SE premiums if relocating, but aiming for £300,000 in Leeds means £15,000 deposit)

- **Liberation System timeline**: Automate £280 monthly (restructured expenses freed £80) + Lifetime ISA bonus £840 annually + protected from £6,000 survey-revealed structural issue through Guardian Framework = £15,000 deposit in 48 months (4 years), but with overpayment strategy and intelligent mortgage selection completes in 18 months by targeting lower entry price (£220,000) requiring £11,000 deposit, achieved in 36 months, then securing Agreement in Principle early and executing quickly

The difference isn't income growth or market luck. It's system architecture.

The Protection-First Philosophy That Changes Everything

Most homebuying advice optimizes for gains: "Here's how to get the lowest mortgage rate." "Here's how to negotiate £5,000 off the asking price." These optimizations matter. But for buyers without parental safety nets, preventing catastrophic losses matters more.

Here's why: saving 0.2% on your mortgage rate over five years might save you £2,000. But buying a leasehold flat with escalating ground rent costs you £30,000 when you can't remortgage. Negotiating £3,000 off the asking price feels like a win, until you discover the £15,000 subsidence repair the survey missed because you hired the cheapest surveyor.

The Renter Liberation System is built on this principle: protection first, optimization second. Every stage includes explicit catastrophic mistake checkpoints:

- **Reveal stage**: Credit score misunderstandings that reduce borrowing capacity by £40,000+
- **Engineer stage**: Depleting emergency funds for deposit maximization, creating house-poverty
- **Navigate stage**: Mortgage products with punitive early repayment charges trapping you for years
- **Target stage**: Properties with cladding compliance issues, leasehold traps, or structural defects
- **Execute stage**: Survey responses that accept undisclosed issues instead of renegotiating
- **Reside stage**: Post-purchase cash flow shocks from underestimated council tax or maintenance costs

Each checkpoint has explicit go/no-go criteria. Not "maybe this is concerning." Not "you should probably investigate." Clear decision rules: if X condition exists, do not proceed until Y resolution occurs. This structure protects you from the expensive mistakes you don't know exist.

What You're Actually Committing To

The transformation from paralysed renter to proud homeowner in 18 months without parental help is achievable. But it's not easy, automatic, or guaranteed. Here's what the system requires from you:

Five focused hours every weekend for 18 months. Not 20 scattered hours destroying your week. Not occasional bursts of activity followed by paralysis. Consistent, protected Saturday morning execution following the structured action plans in each stage.

Complete honesty during the Reveal stage. The system only works if your baseline is accurate. Optimistic assumptions or hidden financial realities will sabotage every subsequent stage. You need truth, not comfort.

Trust in the sequential process. You'll want to skip ahead, start viewing properties before securing your AIP, make offers before implementing the Property Intelligence Filter. Resist that urge. The framework is sequential because each stage builds capability required for the next.

Acceptance that "good enough" beats "perfect." You'll never have perfect information, perfect timing, or perfect certainty. The system teaches you to make protected decisions at 85% confidence and move forward, rather than pursuing impossible 100% certainty and remaining paralysed.

Willingness to invest in professional support where it delivers protection. The cheapest solicitor might save you £300, and cost you £15,000 when they miss a critical lease clause. The system shows you where professional expertise protects your investment and where DIY is safe.

In return for this commitment, you'll gain something more valuable than keys: genuine confidence that every major decision was made well. Not perfectly. Not optimally. But protected, informed, and strategically sound. When you complete, you'll look back knowing you didn't get lucky, you executed a system designed for buyers exactly like you.

The next chapter begins your active implementation. You'll start with Reveal, establishing complete financial transparency and baseline metrics that convert vague aspiration into precise, personalized targets. You'll discover your true starting point, identify your Millennial Buyer Matrix profile, and calculate your exact deposit readiness date.

The waiting is over. The system begins now.

The RENTER Framework, Your Six-Stage Operating System

The difference between homeowners and permanent renters isn't income, it's architecture.

You've likely spent months, perhaps years, consuming homebuying content. Blog posts about mortgage types. YouTube videos on deposit strategies. Forum threads debating London versus Manchester affordability. Friends' advice about when to view properties. Articles explaining stamp duty. Podcasts interviewing first-time buyers. And with each new piece of information, you've felt the confidence drain out of you rather than build. That's not your fault. That's what happens when you treat a sequential system like a buffet, choosing the bits that feel comfortable whilst avoiding the bits that feel hard. The RENTER Framework succeeds where generic advice fails because it replaces information overload with strategic architecture. It's not about knowing more. It's about knowing what to do, when to do it, and why attempting anything out of sequence creates irreversible damage.

The Sequential Architecture That Converts Paralysis into Action

Most homebuying resources present strategies as if they're independent modules you can tackle in any order based on personal preference. They're not. The RENTER Framework is designed as six sequential stages where each one must be completed before the next begins. This isn't arbitrary. It's protective.

Here's what happens when you violate the sequence. You start viewing properties before establishing your mortgage position. You fall in love with a two-bedroom flat in Chorlton priced at £240,000. You spend weekends imagining your furniture in that living room. You research the neighbourhood. You calculate your commute time. You tell your mates you've found "the one." Then you speak to a mortgage broker and discover your actual borrowing capacity is £185,000. The flat was never available to you. You've wasted six weeks of emotional energy and created false hope that now has to be grieved. That's the cost of wrong sequencing.

Or you begin aggressive deposit saving before conducting a financial baseline audit. You cut your spending to the bone. You cancel subscriptions. You stop seeing friends. You sacrifice your quality of life for nine months and accumulate £8,000 in additional savings. Then you finally audit your credit file and discover a default from a forgotten mobile phone contract four years ago that's been silently disqualifying you from every competitive mortgage product. Those nine months of sacrifice? Pointless. If you'd established your baseline first, the Reveal stage, you'd have discovered the credit issue in Week 2, contested it, had it removed within 60 days, and then begun deposit acceleration from a position of truth rather than ignorance. That's the cost of skipping foundational stages.

The sequential architecture exists for one reason: each stage builds irreversible forward momentum toward the next whilst simultaneously preventing catastrophic errors that occur when you operate from incomplete information.

Stage 1 (Reveal) establishes your precise financial baseline, what you actually have, what you actually owe, what you can actually borrow. You can't plan a journey without knowing your departure point.

Stage 2 (Engineer) designs your personalised deposit acceleration architecture based on the baseline from Stage 1. You can't build an intelligent savings plan without first knowing your exact starting position and target amount.

Stage 3 (Navigate) positions you as an attractive borrower and secures your mortgage Agreement in Principle based on the improved financial profile from Stage 2. You can't approach lenders without first having your credit presentation and income documentation optimised.

Stage 4 (Target) activates strategic property search using the precise borrowing capacity confirmed in Stage 3. You can't evaluate properties intelligently without knowing exactly what you can afford to offer.

Stage 5 (Execute) manages the offer-to-completion process on the specific property identified in Stage 4. You can't negotiate effectively or protect your deal without having completed the due diligence frameworks from earlier stages.

Stage 6 (Reside) transitions you into sustainable homeownership using the financial resilience built across Stages 1-5. You can't become a solvent, capable homeowner without having established the emergency fund protocols and cash flow systems beforehand.

The stages aren't suggestions. They're architecture. You don't get to choose which load-bearing walls to keep when building a house. The same principle applies here.

Your Six Stages from Fog to Front Door

Let me show you the complete RENTER Framework with timeline expectations for each phase. This is your 18-month roadmap.

Stage 1: Reveal, Uncover Your True Financial Starting Point (Months 1-3)

You'll conduct a complete financial audit covering every pound you earn, every pound you spend, every pound you owe, and every point on your credit file across all three UK reference agencies. You'll use the Deposit Velocity Calculator to determine your precise monthly savings requirement and projected deposit readiness date. You'll identify which Millennial Buyer Matrix profile matches your situation, solo outside London, couple outside London, solo in London/Southeast, couple in London/Southeast. By the end of Month 3, vague aspiration ("someday I'll own a home") becomes precise, personalised targets ("deposit ready by September 2026, targeting properties at £220,000-£245,000 in Levenshulme and Burnage").

Stage 2: Engineer, Build Your 18-Month Financial Runway (Months 4-9)

You'll evaluate government schemes using the honest assessment matrix that shows when Lifetime ISAs help versus trap. You'll implement the Deposit Velocity System by restructuring expenses into three tiers, non-negotiable, optimisable, eliminable, and automating your savings architecture so it requires zero ongoing willpower. You'll stress-test your runway to ensure you reach exchange with a 3-6 month emergency fund intact, not depleted. By the end of Month 9, you'll have compressed what normally takes 6-8 years into an 18-month timeline through intelligent financial architecture, not monastic deprivation.

Stage 3: Navigate, Master Mortgages and Maximise Borrowing Power (Months 10-12)

You'll execute the three-stage Mortgage Confidence Blueprint: audit current capacity, implement the six specific improvements that increase your Agreement in Principle, secure your AIP at least 60 days before active searching. You'll use the Mortgage Product Shortlist Filter to eliminate 3,000+ products down to three candidates perfectly suited to your LTV band, risk tolerance, and likely ownership period. By the end of Month 12, you'll position yourself as an attractive borrower who can secure competitive products in the top quartile of available rates, converting mortgage confusion into strategic advantage.

Stage 4: Target, Identify, Evaluate, and Select the Right Property (Months 13-15)

You'll apply the five-criteria Property Intelligence Filter at every viewing, structural integrity, leasehold risks, EPC compliance, area fundamentals, investment merit. You'll use the Neighbourhood Fundamentals Scorecard to assess transport connectivity, regeneration pipeline, school trajectories, landlord-to-owner ratios. You'll set automated Rightmove alerts using precision search parameters from your Matrix profile. By the end of Month 15, you'll have identified 2-3 properties that meet your criteria and you'll be ready to make competitive offers without confusing money pits for bargains.

Stage 5: Execute, Make Your Offer, Protect the Deal, and Complete (Months 16-17)

You'll use the Offer Intelligence Protocol to assess seller motivation and comparable evidence before calculating your opening offer. You'll apply the Guardian Framework's ten catastrophic mistake checkpoints at every decision node, survey response, mortgage selection, contract exchange. You'll implement the Deal Protection Checklist to manage your solicitor, surveyor, and broker in parallel. By the end of Month 17, you'll have navigated from offer to completion without career disruption or exploitation.

Stage 6: Reside, Transition Successfully into Proud, Solvent Homeownership (Month 18+)

You'll execute the Post-Purchase Financial Reset Plan within your first 30 days, recalibrating your budget for mortgage payments, council tax, insurance, maintenance reserves. You'll use the Emergency Fund Rebuild Protocol to restore your 3-month buffer within six months. You'll complete the Homeowner Identity Consolidation checklist, utilities transfer, Land Registry registration, insurance setup, maintenance calendar. By the end of Month 24, you'll have established yourself as a financially resilient, genuinely proud homeowner who arrived by strategy, not luck.

That's the complete journey. Notice how each stage builds on the previous one. Notice how attempting Stage 4 before completing Stage 3 creates false hope. Notice how skipping Stage 1 makes every subsequent stage guesswork rather than strategy.

The 5-Hour Weekend Method for Time-Poor Professionals

You're working 45-55 hours weekly. You don't have the luxury of treating homebuying like an unpaid second job. The 5-Hour Weekend Method respects that reality.

Here's how it works. Each RENTER stage is designed to be implemented through focused Saturday morning sessions of approximately 3-5 hours. Not scattered 20-minute sessions across weekday evenings when you're exhausted. Not Sunday afternoons when you're trying to recover from the week. **Structured, protected Saturday morning blocks where you tackle one stage at a time with complete focus.**

Stage 1 (Reveal) requires approximately three Saturday sessions: Week 1 for income and outgoings audit, Week 2 for credit file review across all three agencies, Week 3 for Deposit Velocity Calculator completion and Matrix profile identification. Total time investment: 12-15 hours across three weeks.

Stage 2 (Engineer) requires approximately four Saturday sessions: Week 1 for government scheme evaluation, Week 2 for expense restructuring, Week 3 for savings automation setup, Week 4 for runway stress-testing. Total time investment: 15-20 hours across four weeks.

Stage 3 (Navigate) requires approximately five Saturday sessions: Week 1 for borrowing capacity audit, Week 2-3 for credit and income improvements, Week 4 for broker consultation, Week 5 for AIP securing. Total time investment: 20-25 hours across five weeks.

Stage 4 (Target) becomes ongoing but still operates on the weekend model: Saturday mornings for property viewings, Sunday mornings for evaluation using the Intelligence Filter, weekday evenings only for viewing booking and alert monitoring. You're never taking weekday leave or disrupting your career.

Stage 5 (Execute) requires approximately 5-7 hours weekly for solicitor coordination, survey management, and completion logistics, still achievable through weekend blocks and lunch breaks.

Stage 6 (Reside) front-loads the Post-Purchase Reset into one intensive weekend, then transitions to monthly check-ins.

Total time investment across 18 months: approximately 100-120 focused hours. That's less time than you've already spent researching without a system. The difference is that these 100 hours are strategically deployed rather than randomly scattered.

The method works because it acknowledges a simple truth: you don't need more time. You need better architecture. Five focused hours on Saturday morning with a clear objective and the right tools will deliver more progress than 20 scattered hours across a week spent consuming random content.

Setting Up Your Implementation Environment

The RENTER Framework isn't just concepts. It's supported by a complete tool library that converts abstract knowledge into personalised action plans. Here's what you'll be working with:

The Deposit Velocity Calculator (Stage 1): A spreadsheet template that takes your current income, monthly outgoings, existing savings, and target property price, then calculates your precise monthly savings requirement and projected deposit readiness date across different savings rates. No more guessing. Just mathematics.

The Millennial Buyer Matrix Profiler (Stage 1): A diagnostic tool that identifies which of the four buyer profiles matches your exact situation, then activates the specific strategies relevant to your income level, location, and relationship status. Solo buyers in Manchester follow a different pathway than couples in London. The Matrix ensures you're not wasting time on strategies that don't apply to you.

The Mortgage Product Shortlist Filter (Stage 3): A decision framework that eliminates mortgage products by LTV band, early repayment structure, and rate type suitability, reducing 3,000+ options to three specific products. You'll never again waste hours comparing products you're not even eligible for.

The Property Intelligence Filter Checklist (Stage 4): A viewing template covering structural red flags, leasehold risks, EPC compliance, cladding issues, area fundamentals, and comparable sales evidence. You bring this to every viewing. It transforms you from anxious emotional viewer into strategic evaluator.

The Guardian Framework Decision Trees (Stage 5): Ten catastrophic mistake checkpoints with explicit go/no-go criteria at every critical decision point, survey response, mortgage product selection, contract exchange, completion. Each checkpoint asks: have you verified X, confirmed Y, protected against Z? If no, you don't proceed. That's how you avoid the £30,000-£50,000 errors unprepared buyers make.

The Post-Purchase Financial Reset Plan (Stage 6): A budget template that recalibrates your monthly cash flow for mortgage payments, council tax, buildings insurance, contents insurance, and dedicated maintenance reserves, ensuring you don't complete only to discover you're house-poor and financially fragile.

These aren't optional bonuses. They're core infrastructure. You'll set them up during Stage 1 and use them throughout the entire journey. They're what convert "I should probably save more" into "I need to save £847 monthly to reach my £32,000 deposit target by Month 14."

The Commitment Required and the Transformation Promised

Let's be honest about what this system demands. It requires 100-120 focused hours across 18 months. It requires you to complete stages sequentially even when later stages feel more exciting. It requires you to trust the architecture rather than cherry-picking the comfortable bits. It requires Saturday mornings you could spend doing other things. It requires implementing strategies that feel uncomfortable, like scrutinising your credit file or admitting your actual spending patterns.

But here's what it promises in return.

You'll convert paralysis into action. Right now, you're stuck because you don't know where to start. The framework gives you the starting point, Stage 1, this Saturday, Reveal. That's it. No more scrolling Rightmove at 2am wondering if you'll ever be ready. You'll know your timeline by the end of Month 3.

You'll make decisions at 85% confidence instead of pursuing impossible 100% certainty. The Guardian Framework checkpoints show you exactly what "good enough" looks like at every stage. You'll stop researching and start executing.

You'll avoid the catastrophic mistakes that destroy timelines and cost £30,000-£50,000+. Wrong mortgage products. Money pit properties. Leasehold nightmares. Survey red flags ignored. The framework protects you from all of them through structured decision gates.

You'll compress 6-8 year timelines into 18 months through intelligent financial architecture, not life sacrifice. You'll still see your friends. You'll still take holidays. You'll still maintain quality of life. The difference is your savings will be automated and optimised rather than random and hopeful.

You'll prove to yourself, your family, and your peers that capability outlasts advantages. In 18 months, you'll hold keys to a home you purchased without parental help, without inheritance, without luck. Just knowledge applied systematically. That pride isn't a side benefit. It's the actual destination.

The RENTER Framework isn't magic. It's architecture. And architecture, when implemented systematically, converts impossibility into inevitability.

You're about to begin Stage 1. Chapter 6 will walk you through Reveal, establishing your complete financial baseline, calculating your precise deposit timeline, and identifying your Millennial Buyer Matrix profile. By the end of that chapter, you'll know your exact starting point. And once you know where you're starting from, the path to your front door becomes clear.

Reveal, Uncover Your True Financial Starting Point

You can't fix what you refuse to see clearly.

Most aspiring first-time buyers operate in a strange twilight of partial knowledge, they know roughly what they earn, approximately what they spend, and have a vague sense of their savings. They've checked their bank balance this month, glanced at their credit score on a comparison site, and convinced themselves this constitutes "knowing their finances." It doesn't. This half-visibility isn't neutral, it's actively destructive, creating a distorted picture that simultaneously overestimates barriers and underestimates assets, paralyzing you between unfounded pessimism and unrealistic optimism.

The truth is this: financial fog costs you 12-24 months of your life.

The Audit That Changes Everything

Sarah, 31, worked as a marketing manager in Bristol earning £38,000 annually. When she began her homebuying journey, she "knew" she had about £8,000 saved, spent roughly £1,800 monthly, and probably wouldn't be deposit-ready for another four years. She was wrong on all counts, but she didn't discover this until she conducted the complete financial audit.

The audit revealed £11,200 across four forgotten accounts (including a dormant Help to Buy ISA from 2017 with £2,400), actual monthly expenditure of £2,100 (not £1,800), and a student loan repayment she'd miscalculated by £40 monthly. More significantly, she discovered £340 in monthly "financial drag", subscriptions she'd forgotten, banking fees she didn't need to pay, and money sitting in a current account earning nothing when it could've been in a Lifetime ISA earning the 25% government bonus.

This wasn't a budgeting exercise. This was an archaeological dig through her financial reality.

Here's what the complete financial audit actually entails:

Income Inventory

- Base salary (post-tax, post-National Insurance, post-pension)
- Guaranteed bonuses or commission (use conservative three-year average)
- Side income streams (freelance work, rental income from lodgers, etc.)
- Benefits or allowances (childcare vouchers, car allowance, etc.)

Expenditure Mapping

- Fixed non-negotiables (rent, council tax, utilities, insurance, loan repayments)
- Variable necessities (groceries, transport, phone, basic household)
- Discretionary spending (eating out, entertainment, hobbies, subscriptions)
- Irregular expenses annualized (holidays, gifts, annual memberships, car maintenance)

Savings Archaeology

- Current accounts across all banks
- Savings accounts (including forgotten ones from previous addresses)
- ISAs of any type (Cash ISA, Lifetime ISA, Help to Buy ISA, Stocks & Shares ISA)
- Workplace pension accessible value (rarely advisable to access, but you need the number)
- Premium Bonds, NS&I accounts, or other savings vehicles
- Money held by family members on your behalf

Debt Obligations Clarity

- Student loan type (Plan 1, Plan 2, Plan 4, Plan 5, or postgraduate) and monthly repayment

- Credit card balances and minimum payments
- Personal loans with terms and rates
- Car finance or hire purchase agreements
- Overdrafts and associated fees
- Any informal debts to family or friends

Credit Profile Across All Three UK Agencies

This is where most people make a critical error. They check their credit score on ClearScore or Credit Karma and assume they've got the full picture. They haven't. The UK operates on a three-agency system, and mortgage lenders pull reports from all of them.

Credit Reference Agency	What You Need	Why It Matters
Experian	Full statutory credit report (free)	Used by Nationwide, Halifax, Santander, and most major lenders
Equifax	Full statutory credit report (free)	Used by Barclays, HSBC, and building societies
TransUnion	Full statutory credit report (free)	Used by Lloyds Banking Group and specialist lenders

Access all three. Not next month. Now. You're looking for errors (surprisingly common), missed payments you've forgotten about, accounts you thought were closed but aren't, and most importantly, your actual credit utilization ratio and payment history, the factors lenders actually assess.

Tom, 34, discovered his "excellent" 987 ClearScore translated to a completely different story on Experian, a missed mobile phone payment from 2024 he'd never seen because it wasn't showing on TransUnion. That single error would've cost him access to the best mortgage rates. He disputed it, got it removed, and saved himself an estimated £3,200 over a five-year mortgage term.

From Fog to Formula: The Deposit Velocity Calculator

Once you've completed the audit, you possess something rare: **complete financial truth**. Now you need to know what it means for your timeline. This is where vague aspiration converts into mathematical precision.

The Deposit Velocity Calculator isn't complicated. It's just honest arithmetic that most people avoid because the answer might be uncomfortable. Here's the formula:

Target Deposit Amount = (Property Price × Deposit Percentage) + (Completion Costs + Emergency Buffer)

Let's use Sarah from Bristol as the worked example:

- **Target property price**: £220,000 (realistic for a two-bed flat in BS5)
- **Deposit percentage**: 10% (£22,000) to access competitive mortgage rates
- **Completion costs**: £3,500 (surveyor, solicitor, moving costs, initial furnishing)
- **Emergency buffer**: £4,500 (three months of post-purchase expenses)
- **Total target**: £30,000

Sarah currently has £11,200. She needs £18,800 more.

Monthly Surplus = Total Income - Total Expenditure = £2,310 - £2,100 = £210

But Sarah can optimize. After identifying her £340 in financial drag, her actual available monthly surplus becomes £550.

Months to Target = £18,800 ÷ £550 = 34 months

But here's where it gets interesting. If Sarah uses a Lifetime ISA for the full £4,000 annual allowance, the government adds 25% (£1,000 annually). Over three years, that's £3,000 in free money.

Revised timeline: 28 months from audit completion to deposit readiness.

Sarah went from "probably four more years" to "deposit-ready by Month 28" in a single weekend. The circumstances hadn't changed. The knowledge had.

We have created a ready made Deposit Velocity Calculator spreadsheet for you in Google sheets. Just send us an email to books@fallonpub.co.uk to receive your spreadsheet.

Your Millennial Buyer Matrix Profile

Not all £38,000 salaries face the same market. A solo buyer in London confronts completely different mathematics than a couple in Manchester. The Millennial Buyer

Matrix exists because generic advice is useless advice, you need strategies tailored to your exact combination of income, location, and relationship status.

The Four Profiles:

Profile	Income Reality	Property Price Range	Deposit Timeline	Primary Challenge
Solo Outside London	£30k-£45k individual	£150k-£250k	18-24 months	Income-to-deposit ratio requires aggressive optimization
Couple Outside London	£60k-£90k combined	£200k-£350k	14-20 months	Decision coordination and unequal contribution management
Solo in London/SE	£35k-£55k individual	£280k-£400k	24-36 months	Extreme price-to-income ratios demand geographic flexibility
Couple in London/SE	£70k-£110k combined	£400k-£550k	20-30 months	Balancing commute tolerance with affordability stretch

Each profile unlocks specific strategies. Solo buyers outside London should prioritize Lifetime ISA maximization and consider lodger potential. Couples outside London need joint mortgage optimization and contribution agreement frameworks. Solo London buyers must evaluate Help to Buy equity loan legacy options and consider zones 3-6 seriously. Couples in London/SE should model the commute-versus-affordability trade-off mathematically, not emotionally.

Jamie and Alex, both 29, earning £42,000 and £38,000 respectively, initially searched for two-bed flats in Clapham (£500,000+, requiring £50,000 deposit). When they identified themselves as "Couple in London/SE," they discovered that extending their search to Dartford reduced target property prices to £350,000, cutting their required deposit to £35,000 and compressing their timeline from 40 months to 22 months, while adding only 12 minutes to Alex's commute via Southeastern rail.

This wasn't compromise. This was strategy informed by mathematics instead of aspiration.

The Financial Drag You Don't See

Hidden expenditure is the silent killer of deposit timelines. You think you're saving £400 monthly, but you're actually saving £180 because £220 is evaporating into financial infrastructure you've forgotten exists.

The average UK professional carries £247 in monthly financial drag:

Subscription Creep (Average: £87/month)

- Streaming services across multiple platforms
- Gym memberships for gyms you visited twice in 2025
- Software subscriptions that auto-renewed
- Magazine or news subscriptions you don't read
- App subscriptions buried in App Store history

Banking Fee Waste (Average: £43/month)

- Packaged current accounts charging £15-£25 monthly for "benefits" you don't use
- Arranged overdraft fees
- International transaction fees on cards
- ATM withdrawal charges

Inefficient Account Structures (Average: £117/month in opportunity cost)

- Emergency fund sitting in 0.01% current account instead of instant-access savings at 5%+
- Deposit savings in standard savings account instead of Lifetime ISA (missing 25% government bonus)
- Using credit cards for convenience but not paying full balance (interest charges)

Laura, 33, earning £41,000 in Edinburgh, discovered she was paying £22 monthly for a Barclays Premier account she'd opened in 2019 for travel insurance she'd used once. She was subscribed to Netflix, Prime Video, Apple TV+, and Disney+ (£47 combined) despite watching an average of four hours weekly. Her "emergency fund" of £6,000 sat in a Santander current account earning £0.50 annually in interest.

One Sunday afternoon of optimization:

- Downgraded to fee-free banking: +£22/month
- Cancelled three streaming services, kept Netflix: +£35/month
- Moved £4,000 to Lifetime ISA earning 25% government bonus: +£83.33/month in effective returns
- Moved remaining £2,000 to 5.1% instant-access savings: +£8.50/month

Total monthly gain: £148.83, or £1,786 annually.

This wasn't deprivation. Laura still had Netflix, still had her emergency fund, and still had full banking functionality. She'd simply stopped paying for infrastructure she didn't value.

Credit Score Reality: What Actually Matters

The credit score you see on free comparison sites is marketing. It's a number designed to sell you credit cards and loans, not a number mortgage lenders use. Understanding the difference saves you months of misguided "improvement" efforts.

What Mortgage Lenders Actually Assess:

1. **Payment History** (35% of decision weight)
    - Zero missed payments in past 24 months: strong
    - 1-2 missed payments 12+ months ago: acceptable
    - Recent missed payments: significant damage
2. **Credit Utilization** (30% of decision weight)
    - Using <30% of available credit: strong
    - Using 30-70%: acceptable
    - Using >70%: concern flag
3. **Credit Age and Mix** (25% of decision weight)
    - Accounts open 3+ years: strong
    - Mix of credit types (card, loan, mobile contract): positive

    - Only recently opened accounts: weaker

4. **Recent Applications** (10% of decision weight)
    - No applications in past six months: ideal
    - 2-3 applications in past six months: slight concern
    - Multiple applications: red flag for "credit hungry" behaviour

What Doesn't Matter As Much As You Think:

- Your actual credit score number (lenders don't see it)
- Being on the electoral roll (helpful but not decisive)
- Checking your own credit report (doesn't harm you)
- Having a credit card if you've never used credit (neutral, not negative)

Marcus, 30, spent six months "improving" his credit score from 897 to 956 on Experian by getting a credit-builder card and making small purchases. When he applied for a mortgage, the underwriter never saw that number. What they saw: 100% payment history, 15% credit utilization, four-year account age, and zero red flags. His approval was never in doubt, he'd wasted six months optimizing a metric that didn't exist in his lender's assessment framework.

Your Financial Baseline Dashboard

The final step is consolidation. You've conducted the audit, calculated your velocity, identified your Matrix profile, eliminated financial drag, and understood your genuine credit position. Now you need a single-page reference point you can return to weekly.

Your dashboard should answer these questions instantly:

- **Current Position**: Total savings across all accounts (updated monthly)
- **Target Deposit**: Exact amount needed including completion costs and buffer
- **Gap Remaining**: Target minus current
- **Monthly Savings Rate**: Actual amount being saved after optimizations
- **Projected Readiness Date**: Gap ÷ Monthly Rate = Month X, Year Y

- **Credit Status**: Summary of three-agency check with any actions required
- **Matrix Profile**: Your classification and active strategies

This isn't motivational, it's operational. You're a strategic operator now, not an anxious researcher. Every month, you update the current position and watch the gap shrink. Every decision gets filtered through one question: does this move me closer to Month X, Year Y, or further away?

Sarah's dashboard showed "Deposit Ready: October 2026" in January 2024. By October 2024, she'd accelerated to "Deposit Ready: April 2026" through a £2,000 bonus she'd allocated entirely to her Lifetime ISA and an additional £80 monthly she'd freed up by switching car insurance providers. The date moved because she had the date. Vague aspiration never moves. Precise targets move constantly.

What Comes Next

You've established complete financial transparency. You know exactly where you are, exactly where you need to be, and exactly how long it will take to close that gap. The paralysis that came from financial fog has dissolved into the clarity of mathematical precision. But knowing your starting point is only Stage 1 of the RENTER Framework.

In the next chapter, you'll learn how to engineer your 18-month financial runway, the systematic approach to restructuring your expenses, optimizing government schemes, and automating your savings architecture so that reaching your deposit target requires zero daily willpower. You'll discover why aggressive accumulation doesn't mean monastic deprivation, and how intelligent financial architecture compresses timelines without compressing your quality of life. The revelation phase is complete. The engineering phase begins now.

Engineer, Build Your 18-Month Financial Runway

> The difference between 6 years and 18 months isn't sacrifice, it's architecture.

Most first time buyers approach deposit saving like a punishment: cut everything enjoyable, endure years of deprivation, and hope the maths eventually works out. This belief system keeps capable professionals trapped in rental accommodation for nearly a decade, convinced that homeownership requires choosing between building wealth and living their lives. The truth is fundamentally different: intelligent financial design compresses timelines more effectively than brute-force willpower ever could.

What you're about to build isn't a budget, it's a precision-engineered system.

In Chapter 6, you established your baseline truth: exact income, current savings, monthly capacity, and projected deposit readiness date. That transparency gave you a departure point. Now, in this chapter, you'll design the acceleration mechanism that gets you from baseline to deposit-ready in 18 months, without destroying your mental health, your relationships, or your belief that life is worth living whilst you save.

The Government Scheme Reality Check

Let's address the elephant in the room: UK government homebuying schemes are marketed as universal solutions when they're actually highly specific tools that help some buyers and trap others.

The Lifetime ISA (LISA) is the most powerful scheme for most first time buyers, but only if you understand its mechanics precisely. You contribute up to £4,000 annually, and the government adds a 25% bonus (£1,000 maximum per year). For a buyer saving over

18 months, that's £1,500 in free money. The catch? If you withdraw funds for anything other than a first home purchase or retirement after age 60, you'll face a 25% penalty, which actually takes back more than the bonus due to how percentages work.

When the Lifetime ISA helps: You're certain you'll purchase within 2-4 years, you're buying a property under £450,000, you can afford to lock funds away, and you won't need that money for emergencies. For a 32-year-old earning £40,000 in Manchester planning to buy at £180,000, the LISA is a no-brainer. That's £1,500 in government contributions over 18 months that accelerates the timeline by approximately 2-3 months.

When the Lifetime ISA traps: You might need funds for other life events (career break, relocation, family emergency), you're targeting London properties approaching the £450,000 ceiling, or you're uncertain about your 2-4 year purchasing timeline. A 29-year-old in a relationship that might relocate internationally for work shouldn't lock £6,000 into a LISA when withdrawal means losing £1,500 to penalties.

The Help to Buy ISA closed to new applicants in November 2019, but if you opened one before that date, you can still contribute until November 2029. The bonus structure is less generous than the LISA (25% on up to £12,000, so maximum £3,000 bonus), but crucially, you can withdraw without penalty if plans change. If you've got an existing Help to Buy ISA, continue using it, but don't split contributions between both schemes. The government only allows you to use one bonus, so calculate which delivers more for your specific timeline and commit fully.

Shared Ownership deserves its own honest assessment because it's aggressively marketed to first-time buyers who feel priced out, yet it's the scheme most likely to create long-term financial regret. You purchase 25-75% of a property's value and pay rent on the remaining portion to a housing association. On paper, it looks like an affordability solution. In practice, it's often a trap.

Here's why: You're paying a mortgage on your share, rent on the housing association's share, and 100% of the service charges and maintenance costs. When you want to sell, the housing association gets first refusal and controls the valuation process. When you want to "staircase" (buy additional shares), you'll pay legal fees, valuation fees, and base the purchase price on current market value, not your original purchase price. Many Shared Ownership buyers discover they're paying more monthly than they would for a 95% mortgage on a slightly smaller property, whilst owning less equity and having less freedom.

When Shared Ownership might work: You're buying in London where a 5% deposit on a £400,000 property (£20,000) is genuinely unachievable, but you can afford a 5% deposit on a 25% share (£5,000). You're prepared to accept restricted property rights in exchange for getting on the ladder. You understand you're not buying the property; you're buying partial ownership with significant strings attached.

When Shared Ownership traps: You're outside London or the South East where full ownership at slightly lower property values is genuinely achievable. You're planning to move within 5 years (transaction costs and restrictions make this financially punishing). You value flexibility and autonomy (the housing association controls major decisions). A 34-year-old in Birmingham earning £38,000 who qualifies for a £171,000 mortgage should absolutely buy a £180,000 house with a 5% deposit (£9,000) rather than a 25% share of a £220,000 Shared Ownership property.

The Deposit Velocity System

Now you'll build the engine that compresses your 6-8 year timeline into 18 months.

The Deposit Velocity System restructures your monthly expenditure into three categories: non-negotiable, optimisable, and eliminable. This isn't about judging your spending; it's about identifying where compression happens without deprivation.

Non-negotiable expenses are costs you genuinely cannot reduce without harming your safety, health, or employment: rent, council tax, utilities, transport to work, minimum debt repayments, essential groceries, necessary phone and internet. For a typical first time buyer earning £42,000 in Leeds, non-negotiables might total £1,400-£1,600 monthly. These stay untouched.

Optimisable expenses are costs you need but can restructure for better value: streaming subscriptions (do you need Netflix, Amazon Prime, Disney+, and Apple TV+, or just two?), gym membership (£60/month corporate gym versus £20/month budget chain), food shopping (Waitrose versus Lidl for identical items), phone contract (£45/month for unlimited data you don't use versus £10/month SIM-only). These aren't eliminations, they're intelligent substitutions that maintain quality of life whilst releasing £150-£300 monthly.

Let me show you what this looks like with real numbers:

Case Study: Susan, 31, Marketing Manager, £44,000 salary, Manchester

Susan's initial monthly breakdown:

- Rent: £850
- Council tax: £140

- Utilities: £95
- Transport: £180 (car finance, insurance, petrol)
- Student loan: £120
- Groceries: £280
- Gym: £62
- Subscriptions: £47 (Netflix, Spotify, Amazon Prime, Adobe)
- Phone: £48
- Eating out: £220
- Drinks/socialising: £180
- Shopping: £150
- Miscellaneous: £130

Total outgoings: £2,502 Net monthly income after tax: £2,847 Current monthly savings: £345

At £345 monthly, Susan needed 52 months (4.3 years) to reach her £18,000 deposit target. She didn't need to eliminate joy; she needed to optimise structure.

Susan's restructuring:

- Gym: Switched from premium to budget chain (saving £37/month)
- Subscriptions: Cancelled Adobe (using free alternatives for personal projects), kept Netflix and Spotify (saving £17/month)
- Phone: Moved to SIM-only after contract ended (saving £28/month)
- Groceries: Lidl for staples, occasional Waitrose for treats (saving £65/month)
- Eating out: Reduced from 8 times monthly to 5, chose cheaper venues (saving £85/month)
- Drinks: Pre-drinks at home before going out (saving £60/month)

- Shopping: Implemented 48-hour rule before non-essential purchases (saving £70/month)

Total monthly savings released: £362 New monthly deposit contribution: £707 New timeline to £18,000: 25.5 months

Susan compressed her timeline by 26.5 months (over 2 years) without eliminating socialising, fitness, or entertainment. She still went out. She still had Netflix. She still bought clothes. The difference wasn't deprivation, it was intentional design.

Eliminable expenses are costs you're paying out of habit rather than genuine value: subscriptions you forgot you had, premium services you don't use, convenience purchases that don't meaningfully improve your life. A £9.99 app subscription you haven't opened in six months. The £15 monthly cloud storage for files you'll never access again. The £4.50 daily coffee shop habit that's costing £1,350 annually when a £40 travel mug and office coffee gets you the same caffeine.

These eliminations don't feel like sacrifice because they're not removing value, they're removing waste.

The Automation Architecture

Here's the truth about willpower: it's a terrible savings strategy.

Every month you manually decide how much to save is a month where you're negotiating with yourself. "Well, I've had a tough week, so maybe I'll just save £400 instead of £600 this month." "There's a wedding coming up, so I'll pause saving for a month and catch up later." This approach keeps people renting for 8 years because life always provides justification for delaying.

The Automation Architecture eliminates negotiation entirely.

The setup:

1. **Open a separate savings account** that isn't connected to your current account's debit card. You want friction between your deposit fund and discretionary spending. Monzo, Marcus, or Chase all offer instant-access savings accounts with competitive interest rates. You're not chasing returns here, you're creating psychological separation.

2. **Set up a standing order for payday.** If you're paid on the 25th, your standing order triggers on the 26th. The money moves before you see it in your current account balance. Your deposit contribution isn't what's "left over" at month-end, it's the first transaction after your salary arrives.

3. **Calculate your contribution using your Chapter 6 baseline.** If you need £18,000 in 18 months, you're transferring £1,000 monthly (assuming no LISA bonus). If that's genuinely impossible at your current income level, you extend the timeline or increase income, but you don't negotiate month-to-month. The system runs itself.

4. **Stress-test against emergencies.** This is where most aggressive savings plans fail catastrophically. You save £1,200 monthly for 15 months and reach £18,000, but you've got £300 in your current account and no emergency buffer. Then your car needs £800 in repairs. Or you're made redundant. Or you need emergency dental work. You're forced to withdraw from your deposit fund, pay LISA penalties, and restart.

The protection mechanism: maintain £1,500-£2,000 in your current account as a buffer before maximising deposit contributions. If your monthly savings capacity is £900, don't send all £900 to your deposit fund. Send £750 to your deposit fund and £150 to your emergency buffer until you've got £2,000 accessible. Then redirect that £150 to deposits. This extends your timeline by approximately 2 months, but it prevents the catastrophic scenario where an emergency derails your entire plan.

Case Study: James and Emma, both 29, combined income £68,000, Birmingham

James and Emma wanted to buy a £220,000 house with a 10% deposit (£22,000). Their combined monthly net income was £4,450. After non-negotiables (£2,400) and optimised spending (£1,200), they had £850 monthly capacity.

Their automation architecture:

- £700 to Marcus joint savings account (standing order on 26th of each month)
- £150 to emergency buffer account until reaching £3,000 (achieved month 20)
- After month 20: redirected £150 to deposit fund, increasing to £850 monthly

They opened Lifetime ISAs in April, each contributing £333 monthly (£4,000 annually). The government added £1,000 per person annually, £2,000 total. Over 18 months, they contributed £12,000 from earnings plus £3,000 in government bonuses, reaching £15,000 in their LISAs. Their separate emergency buffer hit £3,000 by month 20. They pulled £4,000 from existing savings they'd accumulated before starting the system.

Total deposit reached: £22,000 Timeline: 20 months Government contribution: £3,000 Emergency buffer: £3,000 (intact)

They didn't eliminate holidays, socialising, or quality of life. They built a system that ran itself, and that system delivered them to homeownership with financial resilience intact, not depleted.

The Monthly Rhythm

Your 18-month deposit acceleration isn't a single marathon sprint; it's a structured monthly rhythm that compounds progress without requiring daily willpower.

Week 1 (post-payday): Your automated standing order has already moved deposit funds. You check your savings account balance, update your tracking spreadsheet, and confirm you're on target. This takes 10 minutes.

Week 2: You review optimisable expenses. Did you overspend on groceries? Are you using the gym membership you're paying for? Any subscription charges you didn't expect? This isn't about punishment; it's about pattern recognition. Five minutes.

Week 3: You check for progress against your Deposit Velocity Calculator target from Chapter 6. Are you ahead, on track, or behind? If behind, you identify the cause (one-off expense versus structural problem) and adjust next month's optimisable tier if needed. Ten minutes.

Week 4: You prepare for next month's payday. Any upcoming expenses that need planning? Friend's wedding, car MOT, annual insurance renewal? You account for these now rather than letting them ambush your deposit contribution. Five minutes.

Total monthly time investment: 30 minutes.

That's the 5-Hour Weekend Method applied to your financial runway: structured, time-efficient progress that doesn't consume your life.

The Timeline Compression Reality

I need to be direct with you: 18 months is achievable for most first time buyers earning £35,000-£60,000 outside London, but not for everyone, and not under all circumstances.

If you're earning £32,000 in Edinburgh and targeting a £160,000 property (10% deposit = £16,000), saving £900 monthly is mathematically achievable and gets you there in 18 months. If you're earning £38,000 in London targeting a £400,000 property (10% deposit = £40,000), saving £2,200 monthly is almost certainly impossible without external help or drastically higher income.

The Deposit Velocity System compresses timelines, but it cannot defy mathematics. What it can do is show you your actual timeline with precision, help you optimise every controllable variable, and ensure you're not adding 12-24 months through pure inefficiency.

The honest timeline framework:

- **Earning £30,000-£40,000, targeting properties £150,000-£200,000 (outside London):** 18-24 months to 10% deposit is realistic with optimisation
- **Earning £40,000-£55,000, targeting properties £200,000-£280,000 (regional cities):** 18-22 months to 10% deposit is achievable
- **Earning £45,000-£65,000 combined as couple, targeting £220,000-£300,000:** 16-20 months to 10% deposit is standard
- **Earning £35,000-£50,000, targeting London properties £350,000+:** 30-40 months to 10% deposit is typical, or consider 5% deposit with higher mortgage costs

Your timeline isn't a moral judgment, it's a mathematical output based on income, target property price, and monthly savings capacity. The Deposit Velocity System ensures you hit the fastest possible timeline for your specific circumstances. It doesn't make impossible mathematics possible, but it does prevent the tragedy of taking 6 years when 22 months was achievable all along.

The Bridge to Borrowing Power

You've now built your 18-month financial runway. You understand which government scheme serves your profile. You've restructured expenses into intelligent tiers. You've automated your savings architecture, so it runs without daily willpower. You're tracking progress with precision, and you've stress-tested your plan against emergency scenarios.

But here's what most first-time buyer resources miss: deposit readiness and mortgage readiness are not the same thing.

You can save £20,000 in 18 months and still be rejected for a mortgage because your credit profile is damaged, your income documentation is incomplete, or your employment status doesn't meet lender criteria. That's why the next stage of the RENTER Framework, Navigate, focuses entirely on your borrowing power.

In Chapter 8, you'll demystify the entire UK mortgage landscape, position yourself as an attractive borrower, and secure an Agreement in Principle in the top quartile of available rates. You'll understand why a 0.3% interest rate difference costs you £4,800 over a five-year fixed term on a £180,000 mortgage, and how to avoid being the buyer who pays that premium through pure ignorance.

Your deposit runway is engineered. Now you'll master the mortgage market that determines whether that deposit becomes keys in your hand, or another year of waiting whilst you fix what you didn't know was broken.

Navigate, Master Mortgages and Maximise Your Borrowing Power

The UK mortgage market isn't designed to confuse you, but it does.

With over 3,000 products from 90+ lenders, each wrapped in acronyms like LTV, ERC, and SVR, the system creates an information barrier that separates informed buyers who secure competitive rates from unprepared applicants who accept whatever they're offered. This barrier is expensive: the difference between a well-selected mortgage and a poorly chosen one can cost £30,000+ over a typical ownership period, even for buyers with identical incomes and deposits. The mortgage stage of your home-buying journey represents your single largest financial decision, and knowledge is the only variable that determines whether you make it well or badly.

Here's what most first-time buyers don't understand: mortgage approval isn't a binary yes-or-no outcome determined by your salary alone. It's a strategic game where presentation matters as much as fundamentals, where timing your application correctly can increase your borrowing capacity by £15,000–£20,000, and where understanding product structures lets you identify deals that save five figures over products that look identical at first glance. You've already completed the Reveal and Engineer stages of the RENTER Framework, you know your financial baseline and you're building your deposit runway. Now you're ready to Navigate: the stage where you transform mortgage confusion into strategic advantage, positioning yourself as an informed, attractive borrower who can secure products in the top quartile of available rates.

This chapter gives you the complete mortgage mastery toolkit, not to make you an expert who could work at a bank, but to ensure you never feel stupid asking questions or powerless accepting terms.

The Mortgage Confidence Problem You're Facing

You've probably already spent hours on comparison websites, opening tabs until your browser crashes, comparing rates that differ by 0.15% whilst having no idea whether those differences actually matter. Perhaps you've used online calculators that gave you five different borrowing estimates, leaving you more confused than when you started. Maybe you've read articles explaining the difference between fixed and variable rates, only to discover each article contradicts the last one about which is "better." This is the mortgage paralysis pattern, the more you research, the less confident you feel.

Here's what's actually happening: mortgage markets are deliberately complex because complexity creates information asymmetry, and information asymmetry allows lenders to price-discriminate between informed and uninformed buyers. The industry doesn't want you to know that two products with identical headline rates can differ by £8,000 in total cost when you account for arrangement fees and early repayment charges. They'd prefer you didn't realize that strategic timing of your Agreement in Principle (AIP) can increase your borrowing capacity without changing your salary. And they certainly won't advertise that specific credit file improvements, taking 45 minutes to implement, routinely increase mortgage offers by £10,000–£15,000.

The good news: you don't need a finance degree to navigate this successfully. You need a structured decision framework that eliminates 99% of available products as irrelevant to your situation, a clear understanding of the six improvements that increase your AIP, and the confidence to recognize that informed buyers routinely secure better terms than desperate ones. That's what this chapter delivers.

The Three-Stage Mortgage Confidence Blueprint

Your mortgage journey follows three sequential stages, each building on the last. Miss any stage or execute them in the wrong order, and you'll either waste months restarting the process or lock yourself into a product that costs you thousands more than necessary.

Stage 1: Audit Your Current Borrowing Capacity

Before you can improve your mortgage position, you need to know where you stand right now. This means getting a soft-search credit check from all three UK credit reference agencies, Experian, Equifax, and TransUnion, because mortgage lenders use different agencies and your score varies across them. You're looking for your actual score, yes, but more importantly you're hunting for errors, outdated information, and financial associations that shouldn't exist.

Sally, a 31-year-old marketing manager in Leeds earning £38,000, discovered during her audit that she was still financially associated with an ex-flatmate who'd defaulted on a mobile phone contract three years earlier. This association, which Sally had no idea existed, was reducing her borrowing capacity by £12,000. A single disassociation request to the credit agencies, taking 15 minutes to complete, removed the link within 28 days. Her borrowing capacity increased from £166,000 to £178,000 without her salary changing by a single pound.

During your audit, you're also calculating your debt-to-income ratio, checking for any missed payments in the last six years, and confirming that your electoral roll registration is current and correct. Lenders use automated scoring systems, and these systems are ruthlessly literal, if your address on the electoral roll doesn't match your address on your credit file by one character, you can be declined for reasons that appear nowhere in your rejection letter.

Stage 2: Implement the Six Specific Improvements

Once you know your baseline, you can strategically improve it. These six improvements are ranked by impact-to-effort ratio, the biggest wins for the least work:

1. **Electoral roll registration at current address** (Impact: High, Effort: 10 minutes), Register at gov.uk/register-to-vote. This single action can increase your credit score by 50+ points.

2. **Credit utilization reduction below 30%** (Impact: High, Effort: Varies), If you're using £2,400 of a £3,000 credit card limit, you're at 80% utilization, which signals financial stress to lenders. Pay it down to £900 (30%) and your score improves significantly within 6–8 weeks.

3. **Closing unused credit accounts** (Impact: Medium, Effort: 20 minutes per account), That store card you opened five years ago for a 10% discount? It counts as available credit that lenders assume you might max out tomorrow. Close it.

4. **Correcting credit file errors** (Impact: High if errors exist, Effort: 30 minutes), Roughly 1 in 4 credit files contains an error. Check for duplicate accounts, payments marked late that you paid on time, and addresses where you've never lived.

5. **Demonstrating savings discipline** (Impact: Medium, Effort: Ongoing), Lenders want to see regular deposits into a savings account, proving you can manage money consistently. Three months of £400 monthly deposits looks better than one £1,200 lump sum.

6. **Income documentation preparation** (Impact: Medium, Effort: 60 minutes), Gather your last three months of payslips, last two years of tax returns if self-employed, P60s, and documentation for any bonuses or supplementary income. Incomplete documentation reduces your offered amount or triggers automated decline.

James, a 29-year-old software developer in Manchester earning £42,000 base plus a £6,000 annual bonus, initially applied with only his base salary documented. His first AIP offered £184,000. After reapplying with full bonus documentation (two years of P60s showing consistent bonus payments), his AIP increased to £210,000, a £26,000 increase from better paperwork, not higher earnings.

Stage 3: Secure Your AIP at Least 60 Days Before Searching

Here's the mistake that costs buyers thousands: they start viewing properties, fall in love with one, then scramble to get mortgage approval to make an offer. This sequence is backwards. You secure your Agreement in Principle before you start seriously searching, because your AIP determines your realistic budget, and your budget determines which properties you should even be viewing.

An AIP isn't a guarantee, it's a conditional promise that, assuming nothing changes, the lender will offer you a mortgage up to a specified amount. It's valid for 60–90 days, which gives you a clear search window. Crucially, getting your AIP early lets you identify and fix any problems before they become urgent. If your first AIP application reveals an issue with your credit file or income documentation, you have time to correct it and reapply. If you discover the issue the day before you want to make an offer, you've lost negotiating power and might lose the property entirely.

The Mortgage Product Shortlist Filter

You're facing 3,000+ mortgage products from 90+ lenders. This isn't a market you can meaningfully compare by opening 3,000 tabs. You need a systematic filter that eliminates 99% of products as irrelevant to your situation, leaving you with 3–5 candidates you can genuinely evaluate.

Here's the Filter:

Filter 1: LTV Band Compatibility

Your loan-to-value ratio (LTV) determines which products you can access. If you have a £25,000 deposit and you're buying a £200,000 property, your LTV is 87.5% (you're borrowing £175,000, which is 87.5% of the property value). This immediately eliminates every product requiring an LTV below 90%, which is about 60% of the market.

LTV bands typically break at 95%, 90%, 85%, 80%, 75%, 70%, and 60%. Each time you cross a threshold, better rates become available. The difference between an 86% LTV mortgage and an 84% LTV mortgage can be 0.3% in interest rate, which translates to roughly £30–£35 per month on a £170,000 mortgage, £10,500 over a 25-year term. If you're close to an LTV threshold, it's often worth delaying your purchase by 2–3 months to save the extra £2,000 deposit that gets you into the next band.

Filter 2: Product Type Suitability (Fixed vs Variable vs Tracker)

Fixed-rate mortgages lock your interest rate for 2, 3, 5, or even 10 years, protecting you from rate increases but preventing you from benefiting if rates fall. Variable-rate mortgages fluctuate with the Bank of England base rate, offering lower initial rates but exposing you to payment increases. Tracker mortgages explicitly follow the base rate plus a set margin.

Which should you choose? It depends on your financial resilience. If a £100 monthly payment increase would force you to choose between your mortgage and eating, you need a fixed rate for security. If you have a robust emergency fund and can absorb payment fluctuations, a variable or tracker product offers lower initial rates. For most first time buyers buying their first home, a 2-year or 5-year fixed rate offers the right balance, predictable payments during the vulnerable first years of ownership, with the flexibility to remortgage when your situation has stabilized.

Filter 3: Early Repayment Charge Structure

Early repayment charges (ERC) are penalties you pay if you repay your mortgage (either partially or fully) before the end of the product term. These charges typically range from 1%–5% of the outstanding balance, which means leaving a mortgage early can cost £2,000–£8,000 depending on your loan size.

Why do ERCs matter? Because life changes. You might receive an inheritance, get a promotion with a signing bonus, or decide to move cities for a better job. If your mortgage has a 5% ERC in Year 2 and you want to overpay £10,000, you'll pay a £500 penalty. Some products allow annual overpayments up to 10% of the balance without penalty, these products are worth paying a slightly higher rate for if you anticipate having extra cash to deploy.

Filter 4: Arrangement Fees and True Cost Calculation

Here's where unprepared buyers lose thousands: they compare headline rates without accounting for arrangement fees. A mortgage at 4.5% with no arrangement fee can be cheaper over a 2-year term than a mortgage at 4.2% with a £1,995 arrangement fee, depending on your loan size.

The calculation is straightforward: multiply the monthly payment difference by 24 months (for a 2-year product), then subtract the arrangement fee difference. If the lower-rate product saves you £40/month (£960 over 24 months) but charges £1,995 more in fees, you've lost £1,035 by choosing it.

Here's a comparison for a £180,000 mortgage over a 2-year fixed term:

Product	Rate	Monthly Payment	Arrangement Fee	Total 2-Year Cost
Product A	4.2%	£923	£1,995	£24,147
Product B	4.5%	£950	£0	£22,800
Product C	4.3%	£933	£999	£23,391

Product B, with the highest interest rate, is actually the cheapest option over 2 years. This is why headline rates alone are meaningless.

Filter 5: Portability and Overpayment Flexibility

Portability lets you transfer your existing mortgage to a new property if you move before your product term ends. This matters because first time buyers change jobs, relocate for relationships, or upsize for families. Without portability, moving house means paying ERCs and starting the mortgage process from scratch.

Overpayment flexibility determines how much extra you can repay annually without penalty. Standard allowances range from 0% (no overpayments allowed) to 10% per year. If you're in a career with performance bonuses, commission, or side income, you want at least 10% overpayment allowance so you can deploy extra cash to reduce your loan balance and build equity faster.

Broker vs Direct: The Strategic Decision

You have two routes to securing your mortgage: applying directly to a lender (like Nationwide, NatWest, or Santander) or using a mortgage broker who searches the market on your behalf. Each route has distinct advantages depending on your situation.

When to Apply Direct:

- Your income is straightforward PAYE (one employer, consistent salary, no bonuses or self-employment)
- Your credit file is clean (no missed payments, defaults, or CCJs in the last six years)
- You have time to research products and complete applications yourself
- You've identified a specific lender product that suits your needs through the Shortlist Filter

When to Use a Broker:

- Your income is complex (self-employed, contractor, multiple jobs, bonus-heavy, commission-based)
- Your credit file has historical issues that need specialist lender matching
- You're time-poor and value outsourcing the research and application process
- You want access to exclusive products not available on the direct market

Brokers typically charge either a flat fee (£300–£995) or a percentage of the loan (0.3%–1%), though many are paid via lender commissions only. The key question: will the broker save you more in better product selection than they cost in fees? For straightforward cases, probably not. For complex cases, absolutely.

Alice, a 34-year-old freelance graphic designer in Bristol with variable monthly income ranging from £2,800–£5,200, was declined by two high-street lenders she applied to directly because their automated systems couldn't process irregular income patterns. A specialist broker matched her with a lender that manually underwrites self-employed applications, securing her a £175,000 mortgage at 4.6%, higher than the best market rates, but infinitely better than being declined entirely. The broker's £500 fee was worth every penny.

Rate Environment Strategy Without Market Timing

You cannot time mortgage markets perfectly, don't try. But you can make intelligent decisions based on the current rate environment without attempting to predict the future. If the Bank of England base rate is 5.25% and 2-year fixed rates are available at 4.8%–5.2%, you're in a high-rate environment. If base rate is 1% and fixed rates are 2.5%–3%, you're in a low-rate environment.

In high-rate environments, shorter fixed terms (2 years) give you the option to re-mortgage sooner when rates potentially fall. In low-rate environments, longer fixed terms (5 years) lock in cheap borrowing before rates potentially rise. The key word in both sentences is "potentially", you're not predicting, you're hedging.

What you're absolutely not doing: delaying your purchase indefinitely waiting for the "perfect" rate moment. House prices appreciate faster than you can save in most UK markets, which means waiting 12 months for rates to fall 0.5% might cost you £8,000–£12,000 in price appreciation, you've lost money trying to save money.

The mortgage market rewards action informed by knowledge, not paralysis hoping for perfect timing. You secure the best product available when you're ready to buy, knowing you can remortgage in 2–5 years when your circumstances or the market changes.

You've now demystified the most intimidating dimension of homebuying, mortgages no longer represent a confusing lottery where you accept whatever terms appear. You understand the three-stage Mortgage Confidence Blueprint, you can deploy the Product Shortlist Filter to eliminate 99% of irrelevant options, and you've learned to calculate true cost beyond deceptive headline rates. You're ready to position yourself as an informed, attractive borrower who will secure terms in the top quartile of available rates, not through luck, but through structured knowledge applied systematically.

With your mortgage capability established and your AIP secured, you're ready for the next stage of the RENTER Framework: Target. In the next chapter, you'll learn to evaluate properties with a strategist's eye, using the Property Intelligence Filter to assess structural integrity, leasehold risks, area fundamentals, and investment merit within a single viewing, ensuring you never confuse a money pit for a bargain.

Target, Identify, Evaluate, and Select the Right Property

The difference between a £250,000 investment and a £250,000 mistake often reveals itself in the first five minutes, if you know what to look for.

Most first-time buyers walk into property viewings with their hearts wide open and their analytical defences completely down. They're scanning for feelings, hunting for that elusive "home" sensation, waiting for intuition to whisper "this is the one." Meanwhile, the property is broadcasting dozens of concrete signals about its true condition, future costs, and investment merit, signals that go completely unnoticed because no one ever taught them the language. This chapter changes that equation permanently. You're about to learn the systematic evaluation framework that converts anxious, overwhelmed viewings into structured assessments, the kind of pattern recognition that typically takes estate agents years to develop, compressed into tools you can deploy this weekend.

By the end of this chapter, you'll walk into any UK property and assess its structural integrity, legal risks, compliance status, location fundamentals, and investment merit within a single 20-minute viewing, never again confusing cosmetic presentation for genuine value.

The Property Intelligence Filter: Your Five-Criteria Defence System

The Property Intelligence Filter is your protection against the single most expensive mistake first-time buyers make: falling in love with a property before understanding what you're actually buying. This five-criteria framework operates as a sequential checkpoint system; each criterion must pass before you invest emotional energy in the next. Think of it as quality control for the biggest purchase of your life.

Criterion 1: Structural Integrity Signals

You don't need a surveyor's qualification to spot the warning signs that separate solid properties from money pits. What you need is a systematic visual checklist that highlights the specific signals revealing whether a building is fundamentally sound or quietly falling apart.

Start at the exterior. Look for:

- **Crack patterns in external walls**: Vertical cracks are often settlement (usually minor), but diagonal cracks stepping through brickwork suggest structural movement requiring investigation
- **Roof condition**: Missing tiles, sagging rooflines, or visible daylight through the eaves indicate expensive repairs approaching
- **Window and door alignment**: Frames that no longer sit square, doors that won't close properly, or gaps appearing where they shouldn't all point to structural shift
- **Damp evidence**: Tide marks on external walls, green algae growth at ground level, or peeling paint near the foundations signal rising or penetrating damp

Inside the property, your checklist expands:

- **Floor levelness**: Walk slowly through each room sensing whether floors feel level, bouncy or sloping floors suggest joist issues
- **Wall condition**: Bubbling paint, dark patches, or musty smells indicate damp problems that cosmetic decoration is attempting to hide
- **Ceiling cracks**: Fine hairline cracks are normal settlement, but wide cracks or sagging areas require professional assessment
- **Window condensation patterns**: Excessive condensation or mould around windows suggests ventilation problems or failing double glazing

Here's what separates strategic buyers from anxious ones: you're not diagnosing the problem during the viewing; you're identifying whether problems exist that warrant further investigation. A single red flag doesn't automatically disqualify a property, but it does trigger the next decision point: is this worth a professional survey, or should I walk away now?

Criterion 2: Leasehold Risk Assessment

If you're viewing a flat, and if you're a first-time buyer in most UK cities, you almost certainly are, the leasehold structure represents one of the most significant financial risks you'll navigate. Yet most buyers focus entirely on the property itself while ignoring the legal framework that governs their ownership.

Your leasehold evaluation has four non-negotiable checkpoints:

1. **Remaining lease length**: This is the single most important number in any leasehold purchase
    - Above 90 years: Generally fine, mortgageable, no immediate concern
    - 80-90 years: Approaching the critical threshold where value starts dropping
    - Below 80 years: Requires lease extension before purchase or immediate extension after, adding £5,000-£15,000+ to your true purchase cost
    - Below 70 years: Danger zone, mortgage availability becomes restricted, re-sale becomes difficult
2. **Ground rent structure**: Read the lease terms carefully
    - Fixed ground rent (e.g., £250/year): Manageable and predictable
    - Escalating ground rent doubling every 10-15 years: Toxic structure that makes properties unsellable, walk away immediately
    - Peppercorn ground rent: Ideal situation, effectively zero
3. **Service charge history**: Request the last three years of service charge statements
    - Consistent annual charges with minor inflation: Normal
    - Sudden spikes or unexplained increases: Red flag suggesting poor freeholder management
    - Major works bills landing on leaseholders: Check the reserve fund status and

planned works schedule

4. **Freeholder reputation**: Search the freeholder's name online with terms like "complaints," "tribunal," or "service charge disputes"
    - Established residential freeholders with clean records: Lower risk
    - Companies with multiple tribunal cases or leaseholder complaints: High-risk ownership structure that will cause you years of frustration

Criterion 3: EPC and Building Safety Compliance

Energy Performance Certificates (EPC) and post-Grenfill cladding compliance might sound like bureaucratic paperwork, but they're actually predictors of your future costs and the property's saleability.

EPC ratings translate directly to running costs:

- A-B rating: Excellent, low energy bills, attractive to future buyers
- C rating: Good, the current minimum standard for rental properties
- D rating: Acceptable, but factor in potential improvement costs if regulations tighten
- E-F rating: Poor, expect high energy bills and potential requirement for improvements before resale
- G rating: Serious concern, may require significant investment to become mortgageable or saleable

The EPC certificate details the specific improvements recommended. Properties where cheap fixes (loft insulation, draught-proofing) would raise the rating are better investments than those requiring expensive interventions like external wall insulation or complete heating system replacement.

Building safety compliance is non-negotiable for flats in buildings above 18 metres:

- EWS1 form confirming no dangerous cladding: Essential for mortgage approval
- Buildings with outstanding cladding issues: Unmortgageable, unsellable, and you may face remediation bills, walk away

- Buildings under five storeys without cladding concerns: Lower risk, but still verify

Criterion 4: Area Fundamentals

The property exists within a location, and that location's trajectory will determine whether your investment appreciates steadily or stagnates disappointingly. Your Neighbourhood Fundamentals Scorecard evaluates four key metrics:

Metric	What to Assess	Why It Matters
Transport Connectivity	Distance to train station, tube station, or major bus routes; journey time to city centre; planned transport improvements	Areas with excellent transport links to employment centres consistently outperform isolated locations
Regeneration Pipeline	Planned developments, council regeneration schemes, new infrastructure projects	Areas in the early stages of regeneration offer the best value growth; areas where regeneration is complete are already priced in
School Quality	Ofsted ratings for local primary and secondary schools	Even if you don't have children, school catchment areas drive family buyer demand and support long-term prices
Owner-Occupier Ratio	Percentage of properties owner-occupied versus rented	High owner-occupier areas (60%+) typically maintain better, appreciate faster, and create more stable communities

You can research these metrics before viewing a single property. For transport, use Google Maps and local council transport plans. For regeneration, search "[area name] regeneration" and "[council name] development plans." For schools, Ofsted publishes ratings freely online. For owner-occupier ratios, estate agents can provide estimates, or you can observe the street directly, well-maintained front gardens, minimal "To Let" signs, and visible resident investment suggest high owner-occupier areas.

Criterion 5: Investment Merit

The property you're viewing isn't just a home; it's an asset you'll eventually sell. Investment merit assessment asks: will I be happy I bought this in five years, or will I regret it?

Three questions reveal investment merit:

1. **How does this compare to similar properties sold recently?**
    - Research "sold prices" on Rightmove or Zoopla for comparable properties (same type, size, condition) in the same area within the last six months
    - Properties priced significantly above recent comparables require strong justification (genuine improvements, better location within the area)
    - Properties priced below recent comparables warrant investigation, is this a genuine opportunity, or is there a hidden problem the market has identified?
2. **What's the likely appreciation trajectory?**
    - Areas with strong transport links, active regeneration, and high owner-occupier ratios typically appreciate at or above market average
    - Areas declining in one or more fundamentals (transport connectivity worsening, regeneration stalling, schools deteriorating) risk underperformance
3. **How easily could I sell this property?**
    - Two-bedroom flats in most UK cities are the highest-liquidity property type, broad buyer pool, straightforward to sell
    - Studio flats, three-bedroom+ flats, or unusual layouts restrict your buyer pool
    - Ground floor flats, properties on very busy roads, or flats directly above commercial premises all face buyer resistance affecting saleability

Setting Precision Search Parameters

Most first-time buyers begin their property search by opening Rightmove, typing in a city name, and scrolling through 500+ listings feeling increasingly overwhelmed. You're going to configure search parameters so precisely that only properties genuinely matching your Matrix profile reach you, converting passive browsing into strategic monitoring.

Your Millennial Buyer Matrix profile (established back in Chapter 6) defines your search boundaries:

- **Solo buyer outside London, £35k income**: One-bedroom flats, specific price ceiling based on 4.5x income multiplier

- **Couple outside London, combined £65k income**: Two-bedroom flats or small houses, expanded price ceiling
- **Solo buyer in London/SE, £45k income**: Studio or one-bedroom flats, specific zones based on transport time tolerance
- **Couple in London/SE, combined £75k income**: One or two-bedroom flats, zone flexibility based on combined commute optimisation

Configure Rightmove and Zoopla alerts using these exact parameters:

- Property type (flat, house, bungalow)
- Number of bedrooms (minimum and maximum)
- Price range (your deposit + mortgage approval determines ceiling)
- Location radius (specific postcodes or travel-time zones)
- Must-have features (parking, garden, etc.)

The goal is simple: when a property matching your precise requirements enters the market, you're notified within hours, not discovering it three days later after five other buyers have already viewed.

Finding the Strategic Overlap: Lifestyle Meets Investment

Here's the tension every first-time buyer navigates: the property you most want to live in rarely aligns perfectly with the property representing the smartest investment. Optimising entirely for one dimension often catastrophically compromises the other.

The lifestyle-only trap looks like this: you buy the beautiful Victorian conversion flat with period features, high ceilings, and character, ignoring that it's on a short lease, has no parking, faces a busy road, and sits in an area with poor transport links. You love living there for two years, then discover it's almost impossible to sell without taking a significant loss.

The investment-only trap looks like this: you buy the new-build flat in a regeneration area with strong appreciation potential, ignoring that you'll hate the soulless development, the tiny rooms, and the 45-minute commute. You tolerate it for three years feeling miserable, then sell for a profit but regret the experience entirely.

The strategic overlap asks: which properties score well on both dimensions?

Properties in the strategic overlap typically share these characteristics:

- Located in established areas with good fundamentals (transport, schools, owner-occupier ratios) where you'd genuinely enjoy living
- Property type with broad buyer appeal (two-bedroom flats are the sweet spot, families, couples, and professional sharers all want them)
- No major red flags affecting either daily life or resale (structural issues, lease problems, location problems)
- Price positioning in the middle of the market range, not the cheapest (often compromised in some way) or most expensive (already priced at peak)

The Absolute Deal-Breaker Red Flags

Some property characteristics are non-negotiable. No amount of price reduction, cosmetic improvement, or emotional attachment can compensate for these fundamental problems. Learning to recognise them instantly saves you from wasting time, survey fees, and emotional energy on properties destined for expensive regret.

Walk away immediately if you encounter:

1. **Leases below 70 years without lease extension agreements in place**: Mortgage availability becomes severely restricted, and extending the lease will cost £10,000-£20,000+ depending on property value
2. **Buildings with confirmed cladding issues and no remediation timeline**: These properties are unmortgageable and unsellable, you'd be buying a liability, not an asset
3. **Evidence of major structural movement**: Severe cracking, significant floor slopes, or structural alterations done without building control approval all indicate problems potentially costing £50,000+ to rectify
4. **Properties in flood risk zones without adequate insurance**: Check the Environment Agency flood map, properties in Flood Zone 3 face insurance difficulties and value suppression
5. **Freeholds with toxic ground rent structures**: Ground rent doubling every 10-15 years makes properties effectively unsellable

6. **Properties with ongoing neighbour disputes or legal complications**: The seller's solicitor should disclose these, but if you hear about boundary disputes, right-of-way issues, or ongoing tribunal cases, these problems will transfer to you

Your Viewing Strategy: Desk Research vs. In-Person Assessment

Time-poor professionals cannot afford to spend entire weekends viewing properties only to discover disqualifying facts they could have researched in ten minutes from their desk. Your viewing strategy separates activities by information source.

Complete before viewing (desk research):

- Sold price history for the property and comparable nearby sales
- Lease length and ground rent structure (usually in online listings or obtainable from estate agent)
- EPC rating and improvement recommendations
- Flood risk, local authority planning applications, and transport links
- Neighbourhood fundamentals (schools, crime statistics, regeneration plans)

Assess during viewing (in-person only):

- Structural integrity signals (cracks, damp, floor levels)
- Natural light levels and room proportions (photos always lie)
- Noise levels (road traffic, neighbours, commercial premises)
- Storage adequacy and layout functionality
- Actual condition versus listing photos
- The "feel" of the building and immediate neighbourhood

A well-prepared buyer armed with comprehensive desk research can often make a viewing decision within 15-20 minutes, because 80% of the evaluation work happened before arrival.

You're no longer the anxious viewer hoping properties will reveal themselves through intuition. You're the strategic evaluator who sees what others miss, assessing value, identifying risks, and recognising genuine opportunities within minutes. This knowledge gap is worth tens of thousands of pounds. In the next chapter, you'll learn how to leverage this evaluation framework to make competitive offers, protect the deal through surveys and legal processes, and reach completion without the catastrophic errors that silently destroy unprepared buyers.

Execute, Make Your Offer, Protect the Deal, and Complete

> Knowledge without execution is simply expensive research that never changes your life.

You've spent months preparing, building your deposit, securing your Agreement in Principle, learning to evaluate properties with a strategist's eye. But this is where the majority of first-time buyers stumble, not because they lack knowledge but because they fail to apply it under pressure. When estate agents push for speed, when sellers threaten to accept other offers, when your surveyor's report contains findings you don't understand, this is when structured decision-making separates buyers who complete with pride from those who either never finish or arrive financially damaged. The execution phase isn't about perfect information or zero risk. It's about making good decisions at 85% confidence while protecting yourself from the catastrophic errors that cost £30,000–£50,000+.

This chapter delivers the complete playbook for the 12–16 week journey from offer to completion.

The Offer Intelligence Protocol

Your first offer sets the trajectory for the entire negotiation, yet most first-time buyers approach it with pure guesswork, either bidding too low and losing opportunities or offering asking price immediately and leaving £10,000–£15,000 on the table. The Offer Intelligence Protocol replaces emotion with analysis, teaching you to assess three specific data points before calculating any number: seller motivation, market time, and comparable evidence.

Seller motivation reveals itself through signals most buyers miss. A property advertised with "chain-free" or "no onward chain" tells you the seller has nowhere to go, possibly downsizing, relocating for work, or in financial distress. This creates urgency on their side, giving you negotiating power. Properties listed as "part exchange considered" or "offers invited" signal desperation. The estate agent's language matters too: "motivated seller" is code for "will accept below asking," while "priced competitively" means they've already reduced once and won't move much further.

Days on market is your second intelligence source. In the current UK market, properties moving quickly typically receive offers within 14 days. If a property has been listed for 30+ days with no price reduction, the seller is either unrealistic about value or the property has hidden issues scaring off informed buyers. Check Rightmove and Zoopla's price history, any reduction in the past 90 days indicates flexibility. A property reduced twice is a property where you can negotiate hard.

Comparable evidence grounds your offer in market reality rather than emotion. Before calculating your opening bid, identify three to five properties that sold (not listed, sold) within the past six months, within a quarter-mile radius, with similar bedroom count, property type, and condition. Rightmove's "sold prices" feature and the Land Registry's price paid data give you this information for free. If comparable three-bed terraces in the area sold for £285,000–£295,000, and your target property is listed at £310,000, you've got evidence the seller is overpriced by £15,000–£25,000.

Here's how you calculate your opening offer using this intelligence:

Step 1: Establish the true market value using comparable sales data. If three similar properties sold for £285,000, £288,000, and £292,000, your baseline is approximately £288,000.

Step 2: Assess seller motivation and market time. If the property has been listed for 45 days with one price reduction, the seller is motivated. If it's been listed for 10 days with multiple viewings, they're not.

Step 3: Calculate your opening offer strategically. For motivated sellers (30+ days, price reductions, urgency signals), open at 5–8% below true market value. For strong-position sellers (new listing, high viewing interest), open at 2–3% below asking or at market value if asking price is reasonable.

Step 4: Leverage your first-time buyer status explicitly. Your offer letter should state: "As a first-time buyer with Agreement in Principle secured and no chain, I can exchange within 8–10 weeks." This is genuine value in the current market, buyers with properties to sell create 3–6 month delays and 30% of sales falling through.

Let's examine a real case study. Emma, a 32-year-old marketing manager in Birmingham, identified a two-bed flat listed at £215,000. Her comparable research showed similar flats sold for £198,000–£205,000 within the past four months. The property had been listed for 38 days with one price reduction from £225,000. Using the Offer Intelligence Protocol, Emma opened at £195,000, 4% below comparable evidence and 9% below asking. The seller countered at £205,000. Emma held firm at £198,000, emphasizing her chain-free status and ability to exchange in eight weeks. Final agreed price: £200,000. By researching rather than guessing, Emma saved £15,000 off the asking price and secured a property at true market value.

The most powerful leverage you possess as a first-time buyer isn't money, it's certainty and speed. Sellers fear chains collapsing, mortgage applications failing, and buyers who "need to sell first" dragging completions into 2026. You offer none of these risks. Use this advantage explicitly in every negotiation.

The Guardian Framework's Ten Catastrophic Mistake Checkpoints

The difference between completing as a proud homeowner versus a financially destroyed one comes down to ten critical decision points where uninformed buyers make irreversible errors. The Guardian Framework installs explicit go/no-go criteria at each checkpoint, replacing subjective judgment with structured protection.

Checkpoint 1: Survey Results Assessment

Your surveyor's report will contain findings ranging from routine maintenance items to catastrophic structural defects. The critical skill is distinguishing between normal wear requiring budgeting and deal-breaking issues requiring renegotiation or termination. Speak with your surveyor to clarify issues

Go criteria (proceed without renegotiation):

- Cosmetic issues: dated kitchen, old carpets, surface-level decoration
- Minor maintenance: cracked roof tiles, garden overgrowth, guttering repairs
- Estimated total cost under £3,000 for all identified issues

Renegotiate criteria (reduce offer before proceeding):

- Major structural issues: subsidence indicators, significant damp, roof replacement needed

- Safety concerns: outdated electrical wiring, asbestos presence, gas safety failures
- Estimated total cost £5,000–£15,000 for all identified issues

No-go criteria (terminate immediately):

- Catastrophic structural defects: major foundation issues, severe subsidence, structural movement
- Post-Grenfell cladding compliance failures on flats
- Japanese knotweed presence without professional eradication plan
- Estimated total cost exceeding £20,000 or requiring immediate habitability work

When Emma's Birmingham flat survey revealed damp in the bathroom and outdated wiring estimated at £4,500 to remedy, she renegotiated from £200,000 to £196,000. The seller accepted, knowing a chain-free buyer willing to proceed was worth the reduction.

Checkpoint 2: Leasehold Term Verification

For leasehold properties, anything under 80 years remaining triggers mortgage difficulties and requires immediate lease extension negotiation, costing £10,000–£20,000. The go/no-go criteria are explicit:

- **Go**: Freehold property or leasehold with 100+ years remaining
- **Renegotiate**: Leasehold with 80–99 years remaining, factor extension cost into your offer
- **No-go**: Leasehold under 80 years unless seller agrees to extend before completion

Checkpoint 3: Ground Rent and Service Charge Examination

Leasehold properties with ground rent above £250 annually or doubling clauses are traps. Service charges exceeding £2,000 annually for flats strain budgets and reduce borrowing capacity.

- **Go**: Ground rent under £150 annually with fixed increases, service charges under £1,500/year with transparent accounting

- **Renegotiate**: Ground rent £150–£250 or service charges £1,500–£2,500, factor into affordability calculations
- **No-go**: Doubling ground rent clauses, service charges exceeding £3,000/year, or evidence of freeholder disputes

Checkpoint 4: EPC Rating and Building Safety

Post-2025 regulations make properties below EPC rating E difficult to mortgage and expensive to bring to compliance.

- **Go**: EPC rating C or above, no building safety issues flagged
- **Renegotiate**: EPC rating D, budget £3,000–£5,000 for improvements
- **No-go**: EPC rating E or below without seller agreeing to remedy, or any post-Grenfell building safety failures on flats

Checkpoint 5: Mortgage Product Final Selection

Your Agreement in Principle isn't the final product. At this checkpoint, you select from your three shortlisted options based on current rate environment.

- **Go**: Product with headline rate within 0.25% of best available for your LTV, arrangement fee under £1,000, and full overpayment flexibility
- **Renegotiate**: Consider paying higher arrangement fee if it secures significantly better rate over your likely ownership period
- **No-go**: Products with early repayment charges exceeding three years, or those lacking portability if you're likely to move within five years

Checkpoint 6: Legal Searches Review

Your solicitor orders searches revealing environmental risks, planning restrictions, and local authority issues. Most results are routine, but specific flags require action.

- **Go**: Clear environmental, local authority, and water/drainage searches
- **Renegotiate**: Minor planning restrictions or historical mining activity with low current risk
- **No-go**: Flood risk zone 3 without adequate insurance availability, contaminated land designation, or major infrastructure planned within 200 meters

Checkpoint 7: Title Deed and Boundary Verification

Title issues discovered late cause completion delays or termination.

- **Go**: Clean title with clear boundaries, no rights of way disputes
- **Renegotiate**: Minor boundary ambiguities resolvable through indemnity insurance
- **No-go**: Unregistered land, active boundary disputes, or unclear ownership of essential access paths

Checkpoint 8: Completion Timeline Realistic Assessment

First-time buyers often agree to unrealistic completion dates, creating unnecessary pressure.

- **Go**: 10–12 weeks from offer acceptance to completion with all professionals confirmed
- **Renegotiate**: Seller pushing for 6–8 weeks, only agree if your solicitor confirms feasibility
- **No-go**: Seller demanding exchange within four weeks unless you're paying cash

Checkpoint 9: Exchange Contract Terms

Before exchanging contracts, verify every term is acceptable. Exchange makes the purchase legally binding.

- **Go**: Contract reflects agreed price, completion date is confirmed, all special conditions are documented
- **Renegotiate**: Any discrepancies between offer terms and contract terms
- **No-go**: Contract containing unfamiliar clauses your solicitor can't explain satisfactorily

Checkpoint 10: Pre-Completion Financial Verification

In the 48 hours before completion, verify your mortgage funds and deposit are ready to transfer.

- **Go**: Mortgage offer formally issued, deposit funds in solicitor's account, all outstanding queries resolved

- **Renegotiate**: Minor outstanding queries with clear resolution path
- **No-go**: Mortgage offer not yet received, or any indication lender may withdraw funding

These ten checkpoints create a decision architecture that catches 90% of catastrophic errors before they become irreversible. At each point, you're making structured go/no-go decisions rather than subjective judgment calls influenced by emotion, pressure, or estate agent manipulation.

Implementing the Deal Protection Checklist

You're working 45–55 hours weekly with minimal weekday availability. Completing a property purchase requires coordinating three professionals, solicitor, surveyor, mortgage broker, across 12–16 weeks without lętting any ball drop. The Deal Protection Checklist gives you the time-efficient management protocol using the 5-Hour Weekend Method.

The 5-Hour Weekend Method structures all purchase-phase activity into focused Saturday or Sunday morning sessions, eliminating the need for weekday calls, emails, or mental energy. Here's the complete implementation:

Saturday Morning Slot 1 (Week 1–4): Instruction and Setup Phase

- **Hour 1**: Instruct solicitor using template letter specifying timeline expectations, communication preferences (email summaries, not phone calls), and requesting weekly progress updates every Friday
- **Hour 2**: Book surveyor for week 3, providing access arrangements and specific concerns from your property viewing notes
- **Hour 3**: Confirm mortgage product selection with broker, requesting formal mortgage application submission within 48 hours
- **Hour 4**: Create deal tracking spreadsheet monitoring solicitor progress, surveyor booking, mortgage application status
- **Hour 5**: Review and respond to any questions from solicitor, surveyor, or broker received during week

Saturday Morning Slot 2 (Week 5–8): Survey and Legal Phase

- **Hour 1**: Review survey report against Guardian Framework Checkpoint 1 criteria, making go/renegotiate/no-go decision

- **Hour 2**: If renegotiating, draft evidence-based offer revision email to estate agent with specific survey findings and cost estimates
- **Hour 3**: Review solicitor's initial legal searches and contract draft, flagging any concerns using Checkpoints 6–7
- **Hour 4**: Chase mortgage broker for formal mortgage offer issue timeline
- **Hour 5**: Update deal tracking spreadsheet, respond to all professional communications from the week

Saturday Morning Slot 3 (Week 9–12): The Exchange Preparation Phase

- **Hour 1**: Review mortgage offer terms against Checkpoint 5 criteria, confirming product matches expectations
- **Hour 2**: Review final contract terms against Checkpoint 9, verifying price, completion date, special conditions
- **Hour 3**: Confirm deposit funds transfer to solicitor with exact amount and timing
- **Hour 4**: Request exchange date confirmation from solicitor, ensuring 2–3 week gap to completion
- **Hour 5**: Prepare completion day logistics: time off work, utility transfer arrangements, moving plans

Saturday Morning Slot 4 (Week 13–16): Exchange to Completion Phase

- **Hour 1**: Confirm exchange has occurred and contracts are legally binding
- **Hour 2**: Verify completion date, mortgage funds transfer, and final payment arrangements with solicitor
- **Hour 3**: Arrange final property inspection 48 hours before completion (optional but recommended)
- **Hour 4**: Confirm key collection process and timing with estate agent
- **Hour 5**: Execute Post-Purchase Financial Reset Plan preparation (covered in

Chapter 11)

This method ensures nothing falls through gaps while requiring zero weekday mental energy. Every professional knows you're available Saturday mornings, expects email communication rather than phone calls, and receives prompt responses within this structured window.

The critical insight: managing three professionals simultaneously isn't about being available constantly, it's about structured availability at predictable times. Estate agents and solicitors work Saturdays. Mortgage brokers respond to emails. By concentrating all purchase-phase activity into focused weekend sessions, you maintain career performance while driving completion forward without delays.

You've now executed the active purchase phase with confidence and protection, making an intelligent offer using comparable evidence, navigating ten catastrophic mistake checkpoints with explicit go/no-go criteria, and coordinating three professionals efficiently using the 5-Hour Weekend Method. The knowledge you've built across nine chapters has translated into irreversible forward momentum. Exchange has occurred. Completion is scheduled. The keys are within reach.

But completion isn't the finish line, it's the beginning of the most financially vulnerable 12 months of your entire homeownership journey. Chapter 11 guides you through the critical first 30 days as a homeowner, establishing the systems, habits, and financial reset that ensure you arrive not just as a homeowner, but as a genuinely proud, solvent one who's built to last.

Reside, Your First 30 Days as a Homeowner

You've crossed the finish line, except it wasn't the finish line at all.

The day you collected your keys; you probably felt a strange mixture of euphoria and terror. The estate agent handed over the keys with a smile, your solicitor sent the completion email, and suddenly you were standing in an empty property that's legally yours, worth more than you'll earn in the next seven years, wondering why nobody prepared you for what happens next. This is the moment when most first-time buyer guides go silent. They've walked you to completion, declared victory, and disappeared precisely when you need them most. But here's the truth they don't tell you: the first 30 days of homeownership are more financially and psychologically demanding than any other phase of your journey, and if you don't navigate them strategically, you risk converting your achievement into a crisis.

This chapter exists because completion is not an ending, it's the beginning of the most vulnerable period you'll face as a new homeowner.

The Reality Nobody Warned You About

Within 72 hours of completion, three things will happen simultaneously: your bank balance will look terrifyingly small, your to-do list will feel impossibly long, and a voice in your head will start whispering that you've made a catastrophic mistake. This is normal. This is expected. And this is exactly why you need a structured plan for the next 30 days.

Most new homeowners stumble through this period in reactive chaos. They discover on Day 3 that they forgot to set up council tax and now face a £200 penalty. They realise on Day 8 that their emergency fund is £1,847 when the boiler starts making concerning noises. They wake up on Day 15 with genuine panic about whether they can actually afford the life they've just committed to. This isn't because they're unprepared, it's because nobody told them that the administrative, financial, and psychological demands of early homeownership require the same strategic approach as the deposit accumulation phase.

You're going to do this differently.

Executing the Post-Purchase Financial Reset Plan

The single biggest shock facing new homeowners isn't the mortgage payment, you've been psychologically preparing for that for months. It's the sudden discovery that your monthly outgoings have increased by £400-£600 beyond the mortgage itself, spread across council tax, buildings insurance, contents insurance, life insurance, ground rent (if leasehold), service charges, and the maintenance reserve you should have been building but weren't.

Here's what your actual monthly increase looks like:

Expense Category	Typical Monthly Cost	Annual Total	Notes
Mortgage Payment	£850-£1,400	£10,200-£16,800	You knew this was coming
Council Tax	£110-£180	£1,320-£2,160	Band-dependent; often forgotten
Buildings Insurance	£25-£50	£300-£600	Mandatory for mortgage
Contents Insurance	£15-£30	£180-£360	Optional but essential
Life Insurance	£15-£35	£180-£420	Protects mortgage if you die
Ground Rent	£0-£50	£0-£600	Leasehold only
Service Charge	£0-£150	£0-£1,800	Leasehold/shared spaces
Maintenance Reserve	£100-£150	£1,200-£1,800	Emergency repairs buffer
TOTAL INCREASE	**£1,265-£2,045**	**£15,180-£24,540**	Beyond your previous rent

If you're staring at that table thinking "nobody told me it would be £2,000 per month," you're experiencing exactly what 87% of first-time buyers report: the hidden cost shock. Your monthly housing obligation hasn't just replaced your rent; it's potentially doubled it.

The Post-Purchase Financial Reset Plan addresses this by forcing you to recalibrate your entire budget before the first payment hits. You're not guessing anymore, you're working from actual figures.

Week 1: Audit and Activate

Within the first seven days of completion, you need to:

1. **Calculate your true monthly homeowner cost** using the table above with your specific figures, not estimates. Ring your mortgage provider for the exact first payment date and amount. Contact your local council for your property's council tax band. Get three insurance quotes and pick one within 48 hours, comparison paralysis costs you coverage gaps.

2. **Set up all mandatory payments** with direct debits scheduled for the day after your salary hits your account. This removes willpower from the equation. If your mortgage payment is due on the 15th but you're paid on the 28th, contact your lender immediately to align the dates. Most will accommodate this for new customers.

3. **Open a dedicated homeowner account** separate from your main current account, and transfer the monthly homeowner total into it on payday. This creates a psychological firewall between "money for living" and "money for housing." When the £1,847 in your main account feels tight, you won't be tempted to raid the housing fund.

Week 2-4: Stress Test and Adjust

The second and third weeks are when reality sets in. You'll discover whether your budget projections were accurate or optimistic. Here's how to diagnose and fix the problem before it becomes a crisis:

Run the 30-day spend audit. Track every single purchase for the first month, yes, every meal deal, every Uber, every spontaneous Amazon order. You're not doing this to punish yourself; you're doing it to see where your money actually goes versus where you thought it went. Most new homeowners discover a £300-£500 monthly gap between projected and actual spending.

If you're running a deficit after Month 1, you have three options:

- **Reduce discretionary spending** in the "optimisable" category: meal subscriptions, streaming services, gym memberships you're not using, convenience purchases that feel small but compound to £400 monthly.
- **Increase income** through overtime, freelancing, or selling possessions you no longer need. A £40,000 salary with 10 hours monthly freelancing at £25/hour becomes £43,000 equivalent, that's an extra £250 monthly after tax.
- **Accept temporary austerity** for 90 days while you rebuild your financial buffer, knowing this is a sprint, not a permanent lifestyle.

The goal isn't perfection, it's solvency. You need to reach Day 90 with your emergency fund rebuilding and your monthly budget in surplus, not deficit.

The Homeowner Identity Consolidation Checklist

Somewhere between collecting keys and Week 2, you need to complete the administrative transition that converts you from "person with keys" to "registered homeowner with functioning systems." This isn't glamorous, but it's the difference between organised confidence and chaotic crisis management.

Essential Tasks, Complete Within 14 Days:

1. Utility Transfers and Account Setup Contact the previous owner's energy supplier (details should be in your completion pack), provide your meter readings on Day 1, and either switch to a better tariff or stay on the existing one temporarily. Set up water, broadband, and TV licence in your name. This feels tedious, but discovering on Week 3 that you're being backbilled for someone else's usage is worse.

2. Land Registry Registration Your solicitor should handle this, but confirm they've submitted the application and get the reference number. You're not legally the registered owner until this completes, usually 4-8 weeks post-completion. Check progress at gov.uk/search-property-information-land-registry.

3. Buildings and Contents Insurance Activation Your buildings insurance must be active from completion day, your mortgage offer required proof before releasing funds. The property price you paid does not correlate with the buildings reinstatement cost. Make sure the buildings insurance does actually cover the cost of rebuilding. Contents insurance is optional but essential. If someone breaks in on Day 5 and steals your belongings, you want to be covered. Get both policies, save the documents somewhere you can find them in a crisis, and set a calendar reminder for renewal in 11 months.

4. Council Tax Registration Register online with your local council within 14 days. They'll send you a bill showing your band, annual charge, and payment schedule. Set up the direct debit immediately, missed payments trigger penalties and damage your credit score, which you've spent 18 months protecting.

5. Annual Maintenance Calendar Setup Create a simple spreadsheet or note with key annual tasks: boiler service (£80-£100, required for warranty validity), gutter clearing (autumn/spring), smoke alarm testing (monthly), carbon monoxide detector checks (monthly), gas safety certificate (annual for leasehold). Schedule these now so they don't become emergencies later.

The checklist isn't optional busy-work; it's the infrastructure that ensures small problems stay small instead of compounding into financial disasters.

Managing Buyer's Remorse and Post-Purchase Anxiety

Here's what nobody tells you: somewhere around Day 7-12, you'll wake up in your new home and think, "I've made a terrible mistake."

This happens to 73% of first-time buyers. It's so common it has a name: buyer's remorse. And it's so psychologically predictable that you can prepare for it, recognise it when it arrives, and manage it without letting it spiral into genuine crisis.

Why This Happens

Your brain is processing three simultaneous shocks:

1. **Financial reality**, you've just spent more money in a single transaction than you've earned in multiple years. Your savings account looks devastated. Every upcoming expense feels threatening because your buffer is gone.

2. **Responsibility weight**, you're now responsible for a £250,000+ asset that can break, flood, burn down, or lose value. When you were renting, the landlord carried that weight. Now it's yours.

3. **Identity adjustment**, for years, you've identified as "someone trying to buy a house." That identity is gone. You're now "a homeowner," and you don't feel like one yet, you feel like an imposter who got lucky and will be found out.

These three forces create a psychological pressure that manifests as anxiety, regret, and the persistent thought: "What if I should have waited? What if prices crash? What if I can't afford this?"

How to Manage It

First, recognise it as normal. You're not having a breakdown; you're having a completely predictable response to a major life transition. The fact that you're anxious means you understand the stakes, which is evidence of capability, not failure.

Second, avoid comparison spirals. Do not scroll Rightmove looking at properties that have dropped £10,000 since you bought. Do not calculate what you "could have saved" if you'd waited. You made the best decision you could with the information you had. Hindsight is irrelevant and psychologically destructive.

Third, focus on what you control. You can't control interest rates, house prices, or the broader market. You can control your monthly budget, your emergency fund rebuild, and your maintenance planning. Channel anxiety into action on controllable variables.

Fourth, give yourself 90 days. The psychological adjustment from renter to homeowner takes three months. By Day 90, you'll wake up and this will feel like home, not a financial prison. Trust the timeline.

If anxiety persists beyond 90 days or prevents you from sleeping, eating, or functioning normally, speak to your GP. Post-purchase depression is real, and it's treatable, you don't have to manage it alone.

The Emergency Fund Rebuild Protocol

You arrived at completion with your deposit, legal fees, survey costs, and moving expenses paid, which means your emergency fund is either depleted or gone. This is the single biggest financial vulnerability you face as a new homeowner, and fixing it is your top financial priority for the next six months.

Why This Matters

Without a three-month emergency fund, the first unexpected expense, boiler failure (£800-£2,500), roof leak (£500-£3,000), job loss, illness, forces you into high-interest debt or panic selling. You've worked 18 months to become a homeowner; you can't let Month 2 destroy that achievement because you didn't have £1,500 for a broken boiler.

The Six-Month Rebuild Plan

Your goal is to restore a £3,000-£6,000 buffer (three months of essential expenses) within six months of completion. Here's the framework:

Months 1-2: Survival Mode (£500-£750 monthly) Your immediate priority is building a £1,000-£1,500 "crisis buffer" that handles small emergencies without triggering debt. This means aggressive spending reduction on everything non-essential. No holidays, no new furniture, no discretionary upgrades. You're in financial recovery mode.

Months 3-4: Stability Mode (£400-£600 monthly) Once you've hit £2,000 saved, you can ease slightly on restrictions. You're not wealthy, but you're no longer one appliance failure away from financial crisis. Continue saving but allow modest quality-of-life spending.

Months 5-6: Resilience Mode (£300-£500 monthly) The final push to £3,000-£4,000 completes your emergency fund. At this point, you're a genuinely resilient homeowner who can absorb normal life disruptions without financial panic.

The rebuild protocol isn't optional, it's the difference between sustainable homeownership and crisis-driven existence. Protect it as fiercely as you protected your deposit accumulation.

You've now navigated the 30 days that destroy unprepared first-time buyers. Your budget is recalibrated. Your administrative systems are functioning. Your psychological adjustment is underway. Your emergency fund is rebuilding. You're not just occupying a property, you're operating as a genuine, capable homeowner who arrived by strategy and will thrive by the same principles.

In the next chapter, we'll extend the timeline from 30 days to 12 months, addressing the longer-term financial rhythms, maintenance realities, and psychological consolidation that transform you from "new homeowner surviving" to "established homeowner thriving." The foundation you've built in Month 1 becomes the platform for everything that follows.

The First Year, From Survival to Stability

Completing on your first property doesn't end the journey, it starts the hardest part.

Most first-time buyers arrive at Month 12 financially depleted, one unexpected repair away from the high-interest debt that undermines everything the 18-month system delivered. The property industry celebrates completion as the finish line, but you now understand it's actually the starting gun for a critical transition period that separates genuinely resilient homeowners from those trapped in house-poverty. This chapter exists to ensure you build sustainable practices that protect the pride you earned at completion.

You're not simply surviving Year1, you're establishing the financial architecture that makes homeownership enhance your life rather than consume it.

What Year 1 Actually Costs You

The month you complete, your financial reality changes completely. Your previous budget, calibrated for rent, accumulating deposits, and strategic deprivation, is obsolete the moment you receive keys. Yet most new homeowners stumble through Year 1 without clear benchmarks for what's normal versus what signals genuine distress.

Sarah completed on a £185,000 two-bedroom flat in Leeds in March 2023. Her monthly mortgage payment was £847, replacing her previous £750 rent. She expected this £97 increase and budgeted accordingly. What she didn't anticipate was the additional £287 in monthly costs that materialised across her first year: £118 in council tax (previously included in rent), £45 for buildings and contents insurance, £82 for utilities now in her name, and £42 for an annual service charge she'd underestimated. Her actual monthly increase wasn't £97, it was £384.

By Month 4, Sarah was using her overdraft to cover shortfalls. By Month 7, she was genuinely panicking, convinced she'd made a catastrophic mistake buying property she couldn't actually afford.

Sarah's experience isn't unusual; it's the default outcome for buyers who enter Year 1 without precise cash flow recalibration. Here's what you need to know: your mortgage payment is approximately 60-70% of your total new housing cost, not 95% as most first-time buyers assume.

The complete Year 1 cost structure breaks down like this:

Cost Category	Monthly Average	Annual Total	Previously Covered By
Mortgage payment	£850	£10,200	Rent
Council tax	£120	£1,440	Sometimes rent, often separate
Buildings insurance	£25	£300	Landlord
Contents insurance	£18	£216	Optional as renter
Utilities (gas, electric, water)	£95	£1,140	Sometimes rent, usually separate
Service charge (if leasehold)	£85	£1,020	Landlord
Ground rent (if leasehold)	£20	£240	Landlord
Maintenance reserve	£75	£900	Landlord's responsibility
Total monthly outgoing	**£1,288**	**£15,456**	**Your previous £750 rent**

This isn't a worst-case scenario; this is baseline reality for a typical £200,000 leasehold flat purchase outside London. If you bought freehold, remove service charge and ground rent. If you're in London or the South East, increase every figure by 30-40%.

The difference between surviving Year 1 and thriving through it comes down to one decision: did you budget using your mortgage payment as the reference point, or did you budget using your complete monthly housing cost?

Execute the Post-Purchase Financial Reset within your first 30 days. Open your current budget spreadsheet and replace your previous "Rent" line item with eight new line items matching the table above. Use your actual mortgage offer, council tax band, insurance quotes, and service charge documentation to populate precise figures, not estimates, not averages from the internet, but your specific numbers.

Then stress-test this new budget against your actual post-completion income. If you're now spending more than 35% of your net monthly income on total housing costs, you're in the yellow zone, manageable but tight. Above 40% and you're in the red zone, requiring immediate intervention through income optimisation or expense reduction in non-housing categories.

James completed on a £240,000 house in Birmingham in January 2024 on a £42,000 salary. His mortgage was £1,124 monthly. He'd calculated this was 32% of his net income (£3,500), well within safe limits. But when he added council tax (£165), insurance (£52), and utilities (£128), his total housing cost reached £1,469, 42% of net income. He was in the red zone on day one without realising it.

James caught this in Month 2 after his first full month of actual outgoings. He implemented two changes: negotiated a £3,000 salary increase by demonstrating market rate evidence to his employer, and reduced his car finance payment by £87 monthly by refinancing to a longer term. These two actions moved him from 42% to 37%, still tight, but sustainable. Without catching this early, he'd have drifted into overdraft by Month 6.

Building Your Maintenance Reserve Without Panic

Your boiler will fail. Your roof will leak. Your consumer unit will trip and require an electrician. These aren't possibilities, they're certainties. The only question is whether you'll handle them from a dedicated maintenance reserve or from a panicked scramble involving high-interest credit cards.

Most first-time buyers enter homeownership with their emergency fund either completely depleted or significantly reduced. You followed the Guardian Framework, so you completed with at least a 3-month buffer intact. But here's the problem: your emergency fund and your maintenance reserve are not the same thing, and conflating them creates the exact crisis-driven borrowing you're trying to avoid.

Your **emergency fund** covers job loss, health crises, and major life disruptions, the catastrophic scenarios that threaten your ability to make mortgage payments at all. Your **maintenance reserve** covers the inevitable property repairs that are expensive but not catastrophic, the £800 boiler repair, the £1,200 roof fix, the £450 drainage issue.

If you fund boiler repairs from your emergency fund, you're slowly depleting the buffer that protects you from actual disaster. By Month 8, you've used it three times for property maintenance, and when you face redundancy in Month 10, you've got £1,800 left instead of the £10,500 you thought you had.

The solution is simple in concept, harder in execution: you need two separate pots of money, built simultaneously, serving different purposes.

Start your maintenance reserve in Month 1, even if you're simultaneously rebuilding your emergency fund. Here's the framework:

Calculate your monthly contribution using property age and type:

- Property built post-2000, freehold house: £50/month minimum
- Property built 1980-2000, freehold house: £75/month
- Property built pre-1980, freehold house: £100/month
- Any leasehold flat with service charge covering major works: £40/month
- Leasehold flat without comprehensive service charge: £65/month

These aren't optional goals, they're minimum contributions. If your property is older, larger, or has known issues flagged in your survey, increase these figures by 50%.

Open a separate savings account, not a current account, not mixed with your emergency fund, and set up an automatic transfer on the same day your salary arrives. The transfer happens before you see the money, before you're tempted to redirect it, before you convince yourself you'll "catch up next month."

Sophie bought a 1930s semi-detached house in Manchester for £215,000. Her survey flagged the roof as having 5-7 years of life remaining and noted the boiler was 11 years old. She set her maintenance reserve contribution at £125 monthly, higher than the £100 baseline because of these known issues.

In Month 4, her boiler failed. The replacement cost £2,400. She had £500 in her maintenance reserve at that point, so she covered £1,900 from her emergency fund with a clear plan: she'd repay her emergency fund first (before resuming maintenance reserve contributions), treating it as an internal loan to herself.

By Month 9, she'd fully replenished her emergency fund. Her maintenance reserve restarted, and by Month 12 she had £625 available. When her dishwasher failed in Month 14, she covered the £580 replacement entirely from her maintenance reserve without touching emergency savings or using credit.

This is what sustainable homeownership looks like. Not perfection, not avoiding repairs, but having the financial architecture to handle them without triggering cascading debt.

Mortgage Overpayments: The Decision Framework You Actually Need

You'll receive conflicting advice about mortgage overpayments from every direction. Some sources will insist you should overpay aggressively from Month 1, treating your mortgage like toxic debt requiring elimination. Others will argue you should never overpay, instead investing the difference in higher-return assets.

Both positions are ideologically driven and ignore your actual circumstances. Here's the framework that accounts for your specific situation in Year 1:

Do NOT overpay your mortgage if:

- Your emergency fund is below 3 months of expenses
- Your maintenance reserve is below £1,500
- You're carrying any debt above 5% interest (credit cards, personal loans, car finance)
- Your mortgage rate is below 3%
- You're planning major life changes in the next 24 months (career move, relationship change, potential relocation)

Consider overpaying your mortgage if:

- Your emergency fund exceeds 4 months of expenses
- Your maintenance reserve exceeds £2,000
- You have no other debt above 3% interest
- Your mortgage rate exceeds 4%
- You're confident in your income stability and location permanence
- Your lender allows penalty-free overpayments (most allow up to 10% annually)

Definitely overpay your mortgage if:

- Your emergency fund exceeds 6 months of expenses

- Your maintenance reserve exceeds £3,000
- Your mortgage rate exceeds 5%
- You have zero other debt
- You're psychologically uncomfortable carrying mortgage debt

Tom completed in June 2025 with a 5.2% mortgage rate. His friends insisted he should overpay £200 monthly to reduce interest costs. But Tom's emergency fund was £4,800 (2.5 months of expenses), and he had £3,200 remaining on a car loan at 6.8% interest.

He ran the numbers: overpaying his mortgage by £200 monthly would save him approximately £42 in interest over the year. Paying an extra £200 monthly toward his car loan would save him £84 in interest and clear the debt 8 months earlier.

Tom chose to ignore mortgage overpayment completely in Year 1. He cleared his car loan by Month 9, then redirected that £200 monthly into rebuilding his emergency fund to 4 months of expenses by Month 14. Only then, Month 15 onward, did he begin overpaying his mortgage.

This is intelligent financial decision-making. Not following rules, but optimising for his actual circumstances using a clear hierarchy: emergency fund baseline → high-interest debt elimination → emergency fund expansion → mortgage overpayment consideration.

Escaping the Scarcity Psychology That Got You Here

For 18 months, you operated in aggressive accumulation mode. Every purchase decision ran through a filter: "Does this move me closer to or further from my deposit target?" You skipped holidays, delayed purchases, optimised expenses, and lived in a state of strategic deprivation designed to compress your timeline.

That mindset was appropriate for the accumulation phase. It's actively dangerous in Year 1 of homeownership.

Many first-time buyers, particularly those who bought without parental help, carry the scarcity psychology straight through completion and into Year 1. They continue living as though they're still saving for a deposit, refusing quality-of-life expenses, feeling guilty about any discretionary spending, and measuring success purely through savings account growth.

The result is house-poverty: owning property but experiencing life quality worse than when you were renting. You're technically a homeowner, but you're miserable, isolated, and building resentment toward the house that was supposed to represent achievement and pride.

Here's what you need to understand: **homeownership should enhance your life, not consume it.** If you're more financially stressed, socially isolated, and psychologically depleted in Month 12 than you were in Month 1 of your deposit accumulation journey, something is broken in your approach.

The transition from accumulation mode to sustainable homeowner equilibrium requires conscious recalibration. You're no longer racing toward a finish line, you've crossed it. The new goal is building long-term resilience and wealth while maintaining quality of life.

This means permitting yourself to resume activities and purchases that bring genuine value to your life. Not reckless spending, not abandoning financial discipline, but recognising that sustainable homeownership includes actually enjoying the life you've worked impossibly hard to create.

Rachel completed in August 2023 after 19 months of aggressive saving. She'd cut her social spending to nearly zero during accumulation, skipping friends' birthday dinners, avoiding weekend trips, and eliminating her gym membership. By completion, she'd saved £32,000, but she'd also isolated herself socially and gained 18 pounds from stress and reduced activity.

In Month 3 of homeownership, Rachel was still living in full deprivation mode. She had £8,500 in combined emergency fund and maintenance reserve, zero debt, and was saving £890 monthly. But she was profoundly unhappy, and her friendships had deteriorated to the point where invitations had stopped coming.

Her turning point came in Month 5 when she realised she was optimising for numbers on a spreadsheet while her actual life quality was collapsing. She made three deliberate changes: she resumed her gym membership (£42/month), she allocated £120/month for social activities with clear boundaries, and she booked a long weekend trip she'd been postponing for two years (£380 total).

These changes reduced her monthly savings from £890 to £728, still substantial, still building wealth, but no longer at the expense of her health and relationships. By Month 12, Rachel's savings had grown by £8,736 instead of the £10,680 she'd have achieved in full deprivation mode. But her life satisfaction, physical health, and social connections had recovered completely.

She traded £1,944 in additional savings for getting her life back. That's not financial irresponsibility, that's intelligent optimisation for actual wellbeing rather than spreadsheet performance.

When Housing Stability Changes Your Career Calculus

Homeownership fundamentally shifts your career decision-making in ways you won't immediately recognise. As a renter, every professional choice carried underlying housing precarity: "If this doesn't work out, will I be able to afford rent increases?" "If I take a lower-paying role to change industries, will I get priced out of my area?"

Housing stability removes these calculations. You've fixed your largest monthly expense for the next 2-5 years (your mortgage deal term). This security enables professional risks that were genuinely impossible as a perpetual renter.

Consider salary negotiations. As a renter, aggressive negotiation carried real risk: push too hard, relationship deteriorates, you're job-hunting in 6 months while facing rent increases. As a homeowner with 18 months of expenses in combined emergency fund and equity, you negotiate from a position of genuine strength. You can walk away from inadequate offers because your housing cost is stable.

Marcus completed in April 2024. In Month 8, he received a job offer from a competitor offering £7,000 more annually. As a renter, he'd have accepted immediately, the income increase was too substantial to risk. But as a homeowner with housing stability, Marcus used the offer as leverage with his current employer, who countered with a £6,500 increase plus clearer promotion pathway. He stayed, negotiated from strength, and achieved 90% of the gain without the disruption of changing companies.

Homeownership also enables calculated industry changes and entrepreneurial ventures. If you're considering moving from corporate employment to freelancing, or from a stable industry to a growing but volatile one, housing cost stability is the foundation that makes the risk manageable.

The framework is simple: if your emergency fund covers 6+ months of expenses and your mortgage is fixed for 3+ years, you have a genuine runway for professional experimentation that simply didn't exist as a renter facing annual rent increases.

Measuring Year 1 Success Using Appropriate Benchmarks

By Month 12, you need to assess whether you've successfully transitioned from first-time buyer into resilient homeowner. But the metrics that matter have nothing to do with property value appreciation or mortgage balance reduction.

Here are the six success indicators for Year 1:

1. Payment Consistency: You've made every mortgage payment on time without using overdraft or credit to cover shortfalls.

2. Emergency Fund Status: Your emergency fund equals or exceeds 3 months of expenses, rebuilt if it was depleted during purchase.

3. Maintenance Reserve Growth: You have £1,200+ in dedicated maintenance reserve, separate from emergency savings.

4. Debt Position: You have no new high-interest debt incurred during Year 1, and existing debt has either remained stable or decreased.

5. Quality of Life Maintenance: You've maintained social connections, physical health, and mental wellbeing; you're not house poor.

6. Confidence Level: You feel genuinely proud of your homeownership status and confident in your ability to handle Year 2, not anxious and regretful.

If you've achieved 5-6 of these indicators, you've successfully transitioned into sustainable homeownership. If you've achieved 3-4, you're on track but need to strengthen specific areas. Below 3 indicates you need immediate intervention, likely through income optimisation, expense restructuring, or seeking professional financial guidance.

Year 1 isn't about perfection. It's about establishing the financial practices and psychological equilibrium that ensure homeownership enhances your life rather than consuming it. You've proven you're capable of achieving what the system told you was impossible. Year 1 is where you prove you can sustain it.

In the next chapter, we'll address the specific strategies for solo buyers navigating homeownership entirely alone, the unique challenges you face, the distinct advantages you possess, and the support systems that ensure you thrive rather than simply survive.

Solo Buyer Strategies, Navigating Homeownership Alone

> Buying property alone isn't a consolation prize, it's a strategic position of power.

The cultural narrative surrounding solo homebuying is poisonous: you buy alone because you "have to," because you're "still single," because you haven't yet found someone to share the burden. This framing treats solo purchasing as a second-tier pathway requiring apology rather than what it actually represents, complete decision autonomy, absolute financial control, and relationship-proof ownership that cannot be undermined by breakups, disagreements, or the power imbalances that joint ownership creates. Your single salary isn't a limitation to overcome through wishful thinking or delayed timelines. It's a constraint that forces intelligent optimization, and intelligent optimization produces better long-term outcomes than the complacent compromises that abundant capital enables. Solo buyers who understand this truth don't just achieve homeownership, they build foundations that coupled buyers, navigating constant negotiation and compromise, can never replicate.

The Solo Buyer Advantage Nobody Talks About

Decision autonomy is worth more than most people realize. When you buy alone, every choice point in the RENTER Framework belongs entirely to you. You don't negotiate property types with a partner who wants a garden when you value location. You don't compromise on neighbourhoods because their commute matters as much as yours. You don't delay searching because they're "not quite ready yet" or accelerate because they're pressuring for timeline compression you can't sustain. The offer you make, the survey issues you accept or reject, the completion date you target, these decisions execute at the speed of your own conviction, not the lowest common denominator of joint agreement.

Complete financial control extends beyond decision speed. Your deposit is yours. Your mortgage payments reflect your income alone. Your emergency fund rebuilds according to your risk tolerance, not someone else's spending patterns. If you choose to overpay the mortgage aggressively in Year 2, you do. If you prioritize quality of life and minimum payments while rebuilding savings, you do. There's no negotiation, no resentment about unequal contributions, no silent scorekeeping about who sacrificed more during the deposit accumulation phase.

Relationship-proof ownership means the property cannot be weaponized. Breakups don't force sales. Relationship deterioration doesn't trap you in joint ownership with someone you can barely speak to. Future partnerships begin from a position of asset clarity rather than property entanglement that preceded the relationship. You own this. Completely. The Land Registry knows it. Your mortgage lender knows it. And every future romantic partner will enter your life understanding that your housing security doesn't depend on them.

Income Optimization When There's Only One Salary

Single-salary homebuying requires precision that coupled buyers never develop. The geographic radius expansion strategy is your first lever. In London, a single £45,000 salary gets you nothing viable in Zones 1-2. But that same salary, combined with willingness to accept a 45-minute commute, unlocks Zone 4 properties that coupled buyers overlook because "we don't want to be that far out." You're not compromising, you're arbitraging the premium that proximity-obsessed buyers pay for 15 minutes of commute reduction.

Property type flexibility is your second advantage. Coupled buyers default to two-bedroom requirements because "we need space for guests" or "what if we have children." You can access one-bedroom properties that offer significantly better value per square foot, stronger investment fundamentals in city-centre locations, and faster appreciation because first-time buyer demand concentrates in the one-bed sector. The couple paying £320,000 for a two-bed ex-council flat in Zone 3 could be you paying £245,000 for a one-bed conversion in Zone 2, better location, newer build, stronger appreciation trajectory.

The Shared Ownership calculation changes for solo buyers. For couples, Shared Ownership often fails the mathematical test because combined salaries can access full ownership at similar monthly costs through standard mortgages. For solo buyers earning £35,000-£42,000 in London or the South East, Shared Ownership can be the only viable pathway to ownership in a reasonable location. The key is treating it as what it is, a 5-7 year stepping stone, not a permanent solution. You buy 25-40% of a property, build equity while rent levels remain controlled, staircase to majority ownership once income increases, then sell and move to full ownership elsewhere.

Income-to-Property Price Optimization by UK Region

Location	Solo Income	Realistic Budget	Property Type	Timeline to Deposit
Birmingham	£32,000	£140,000-£160,000	1-bed flat, emerging areas	14 months (£12k deposit, LISA)
Manchester	£38,000	£160,000-£185,000	1-bed flat, Ancoats/Northern Quarter	16 months (£14k deposit, LISA)
Leeds	£35,000	£145,000-£170,000	1-bed flat, city centre fringe	15 months (£13k deposit, LISA)
Bristol	£42,000	£190,000-£220,000	1-bed flat, Bedminster/Southville	18 months (£17k deposit, LISA)
Edinburgh	£40,000	£175,000-£200,000	1-bed flat, Leith/Stockbridge	17 months (£16k deposit, LISA)
London Zone 4	£45,000	£260,000-£290,000	1-bed flat or Shared Ownership 2-bed	22 months (£20k deposit, LISA) or SO entry

These aren't aspirational figures requiring perfect execution. They're systematic outcomes when solo buyers apply income optimization without the compromise drag that couples introduce. Notice the consistent LISA deployment, the government adds 25% to your contributions, and when there's only one person's savings to coordinate, you maximize the £4,000 annual contribution without negotiation.

Building Your Support Architecture Without Creating Dependency

Solo buyers need structured support systems that coupled buyers get automatically. Your support network requires three distinct layers, each serving specific functions without creating uncomfortable obligation or dependency.

Layer 1: Professional expertise for high-stakes decisions. This isn't optional, it's protection. You hire a mortgage broker for product selection and AIP positioning (£300-£500). You hire a solicitor for conveyancing (£1,000-£1,500). You hire a surveyor for structural assessment (£400-£600 depending on property type). These aren't relationship favours you're calling in, they're paid professional services where the expert carries professional indemnity insurance and you maintain client-service provider boundaries. When your survey reveals subsidence, you're not asking a friend whether to proceed, you're instructing a qualified professional whose advice you can rely on legally.

Layer 2: Skilled assistance for practical tasks. You identify 2-3 trusted individuals, friends, family members, colleagues, who can provide specific practical help during viewings, move coordination, or early maintenance tasks. The framework here is explicit reciprocity: you're not asking for free labour, you're exchanging value. They help you move, you help them move. They accompany you to viewings for second opinions, you return the favour when they're car shopping. They show you how to bleed radiators, you cook them dinner. The exchange is clear, bounded, and reciprocal, this prevents resentment and maintains relationship health.

Layer 3: Emotional support from people who understand the journey. You cultivate relationships with at least two people who've recently bought property themselves, ideally solo buyers who've navigated the same psychological terrain. These aren't professional relationships or transactional exchanges. They're genuine friendships where you can process the 3am anxiety, the buyer's remorse in Week 2, the isolation of carrying full responsibility alone. You find these people through first-time buyer forums, through colleagues who've recently completed, through extended social networks. The conversation isn't advice-seeking, it's validation-seeking. "Is it normal to feel terrified in Week 3?" "Yes. I felt that too. It passes."

Managing the Psychological Weight of Solo Ownership

The emotional reality of solo homeownership is complex in ways that coupled buyers never experience. The pride is fiercer because you've proved capability without partnership cushioning. The isolation is sharper because there's nobody to share the 2am leak anxiety or the boiler replacement decision. The responsibility is heavier because every mortgage payment, every maintenance cost, every financial decision lands entirely on you.

Pride management means permitting yourself to feel genuinely accomplished without minimizing the achievement. You didn't buy because someone helped you financially. You didn't buy because dual incomes made it easy. You compressed a 6-8 year timeline to 18 months through systematic execution of the RENTER Framework using only your own income, your own discipline, your own strategic intelligence. That's worth celebrating. Tell people. Post the photo. Feel the satisfaction. Too many solo buyers downplay their success because they're conditioned to think homeownership "doesn't count" unless you're coupled. Reject that conditioning.

Isolation management requires building check-in systems for the practical and psychological challenges. You set calendar reminders for quarterly property maintenance checks, not because you'll forget, but because the reminder externalizes responsibility and reduces mental load. You join the neighbourhood WhatsApp group or residents' association not because you love community admin, but because it creates connection points that prevent complete housing isolation. You maintain at least one regular social commitment that gets you out of the property weekly, because solo homeownership can become solo isolation if you're not intentional.

Responsibility management means accepting that you'll make some mistakes and building financial resilience to absorb them. Your emergency fund target isn't 3 months of expenses, it's 6 months, because you don't have a partner's income to bridge gaps if you lose your job. Your maintenance reserve isn't optional, it's mandatory, because unexpected boiler failures can't wait until next month's payday. Your decision-making process includes a 48-hour cooling-off period for any financial commitment over £500, because you're the only check on impulsive decisions.

The DIY Versus Professional Decision Framework

Solo buyers face a persistent tension: DIY saves money but requires time and skill, while professional help protects outcomes but depletes cash reserves. The framework for making these decisions intelligently is clearer than most people realize.

Always DIY: Cosmetic improvements (painting, decorating), basic maintenance you can learn via YouTube in under 30 minutes (bleeding radiators, replacing tap washers, changing light fixtures), flat-pack furniture assembly, garden maintenance, cleaning and organization.

Always professional: Anything involving gas (boiler servicing, gas appliance installation), electrical work requiring Part P certification, structural alterations, damp treatment, roof repairs, anything where failure creates safety hazards or voids insurance, anything where the cost of getting it wrong exceeds 3x the cost of professional help.

Evaluate case-by-case: Plumbing repairs beyond washer replacement, appliance installation, minor carpentry, fence repairs, minor plastering. The decision framework here is simple: if you possess the skill and the task takes under 4 hours, DIY. If you don't possess the skill but can learn it in under 2 hours via quality tutorials and the task isn't time-sensitive, DIY and skill-build. If the task is time-sensitive, requires skills you don't have, or failure would cause damage exceeding £200, hire professionals.

Protecting Your Asset While Remaining Open to Partnership

Future relationship considerations require explicit legal and strategic frameworks that coupled buyers never develop because they're already in relationships. You're protecting an asset you built alone while maintaining openness to partnership, these goals aren't contradictory if you structure them correctly.

If you enter a serious relationship post-purchase, you establish beneficial interest protection before cohabitation begins. This is a formal declaration, drafted by a solicitor, confirming that the property is your sole asset and any future partner living with you has no equity claim regardless of contribution to bills or maintenance. This isn't pessimistic, it's protective. The relationship might be perfect, but you're protecting yourself and them from messy legal disputes if it ends.

If the relationship progresses to marriage consideration, you discuss pre-nuptial agreements that explicitly protect the property as pre-marital sole ownership. Modern family law increasingly recognizes pre-nups if they're fair, properly drafted, and both parties have independent legal advice. This isn't romance-killing, it's grown-up financial planning that protects both people's interests clearly.

If you eventually want to transition the property into joint ownership with a long-term partner, you structure it as a formal sale of equity share at market value, not a gift. They buy into the property at current market rates, proportional to the equity share you're transferring. This maintains fairness, creates clean legal records, and ensures you're compensated for the appreciation you've built alone.

Three Solo Buyers: Income, Geography, Strategy, Outcome

Case Study 1: Maya, £32,000, Birmingham, 14 Months to Completion

Maya earned £32,000 as a marketing coordinator in Birmingham, had £4,500 in existing savings, and carried £22,000 in student loan debt. She opened a Lifetime ISA immediately and maximized contributions at £333 monthly (£4,000 annually), receiving £1,000 government bonus. She restructured discretionary spending, eliminating £180 monthly in subscription services and unused gym memberships, increasing deposit savings to £520 monthly.

Her geographic optimization focused on emerging Birmingham areas, Digbeth and Balsall Heath, where one-bedroom flats traded at £140,000-£155,000 versus £180,000+ in established Jewellery Quarter. She secured a mortgage Agreement in Principle at 4.5x salary (£144,000) after improving credit score from 720 to 798 through clearing an old mobile phone debt and registering on the electoral roll.

After 14 months, she'd accumulated £11,800 in savings plus £2,950 in LISA bonuses (£14,750 total). She purchased a one-bedroom flat in Digbeth for £148,000, using a 10% deposit (£14,800), with mortgage of £133,200. Her monthly mortgage payment was £710. She completed without family financial assistance, built a 3-month emergency fund within 7 months post-purchase, and achieved 18% property appreciation within 24 months as Digbeth regeneration accelerated.

Case Study 2: David, £45,000, Manchester, 16 Months to Completion

David earned £45,000 as a software developer in Manchester, had £8,000 in existing savings, no debt, and excellent credit (812). He maximized LISA contributions at £333 monthly and saved an additional £450 monthly through aggressive expense optimization including moving to a cheaper house-share (reducing rent from £850 to £650).

His property strategy targeted Ancoats and New Islington, areas with new-build one-bedroom flats offering Help to Buy equity loans (though the scheme had ended, resale properties with existing loans remained available). He secured a 4.75x income mortgage (£213,750) and focused on properties around £185,000-£195,000.

After 16 months, he'd accumulated £15,200 in savings plus £3,800 in LISA bonuses (£19,000 total). He purchased a one-bedroom new-build flat in Ancoats for £189,000 using a 10% deposit (£18,900), with mortgage of £170,100. His monthly mortgage payment was £895. The property included access to communal gym and co-working space, reducing his external costs. He maintained quality of life while building equity, proving solo buying doesn't require miserable deprivation.

Case Study 3: Aisha, £52,000, London Zone 4, 22 Months via Shared Ownership

Aisha earned £52,000 as a senior analyst in London, had £6,500 in existing savings, and £18,000 in student loan debt. Her income qualified her for £234,000 mortgage (4.5x), but London property prices made full ownership impossible in acceptable locations. She evaluated Shared Ownership in Zone 4 (Walthamstow, Leytonstone) where two-bedroom properties valued at £425,000 offered 40% shares.

She maximized LISA contributions (£333 monthly) and saved an additional £380 monthly. After 22 months, she'd accumulated £15,700 in savings plus £3,925 in LISA bonuses (£19,625 total). She purchased a 40% share (£170,000) of a two-bedroom flat valued at £425,000 in Walthamstow, using a 10% deposit on her share (£17,000), with mortgage of £153,000 on her portion. Her monthly costs were £805 mortgage plus £456 rent on the 60% she didn't own (£1,261 total), comparable to renting alone but building equity.

Her strategy involved staircasing: as income increased to £58,000 by Year 3, she purchased an additional 25% share, reaching 65% ownership. By Year 5, she sold the Shared Ownership property at 15% appreciation, extracted her equity, and bought a one-bedroom flat in Zone 3 with full ownership. Shared Ownership wasn't permanent; it was strategic entry into London homeownership that solo income enabled.

These three buyers prove what income-specific optimization achieves: solo buyers at different salary levels, in different UK cities, all completing within 14-22 months using systematic RENTER Framework execution. They didn't wait for relationships. They didn't wait for inheritances. They didn't wait for impossible income growth. They applied knowledge, structured their finances intelligently, optimized for their geographic and income reality, and achieved homeownership that remains secure regardless of relationship status.

In the next chapter, we'll examine the opposite pathway, joint purchasing for couples, and the specific legal, financial, and relationship frameworks required to navigate homeownership together without creating resentment, vulnerability, or financial entanglement that outlasts the relationship itself.

Couple Strategies, Joint Purchase Without the Mess

> Joint homebuying without legal protection creates the vulnerability you're trying to escape.

Most couples approach their first property purchase with a dangerous mix of optimism and avoidance, believing that discussing legal structures, unequal contributions, and breakup scenarios signals relationship weakness when it actually demonstrates mature commitment. You've watched friends buy together with nothing more than verbal agreements and crossed fingers, only to discover years later that a single unchecked box on a form has created catastrophic financial exposure neither person understood. The truth that mortgage brokers and conveyancing solicitors rarely explain clearly: joint ownership without explicit protection frameworks doesn't strengthen relationships, it creates precisely the power imbalances, resentment, and financial traps you're working so hard to avoid.

This chapter eliminates the guesswork that destroys couples during the buying process.

The Two Paths That Determine Everything

The legal structure you choose at purchase, a single decision made in a solicitor's office, controls what happens to your property when one person dies, when you separate, or when you want to sell. Most couples select joint tenancy by default because it sounds equal and romantic, without understanding they've just signed away critical protections that can never be reinstated without remortgaging.

Joint tenants means you both own 100% of the property together as a single legal entity. When one person dies, their share automatically transfers to the surviving partner regardless of what their will says, this is called the "right of survivorship." It sounds protective until you realise it also means:

- Neither person can leave their share to children from previous relationships
- You cannot specify different ownership percentages based on who contributed what
- If one person faces bankruptcy or legal judgment, the entire property is at risk
- Selling requires unanimous agreement, one person cannot force a sale alone

Tenants in common means you each own a specific percentage of the property that you define at purchase (typically matching your deposit contributions). When one person dies, their share passes according to their will, not automatically to the co-owner. This structure means:

- Unequal contributors are protected through documented percentage ownership
- Each person can leave their share to whoever they choose
- One person's financial problems affect only their percentage, not the whole property
- Either person can theoretically force a sale through court (though this requires legal action)

Here's what solicitors won't tell you clearly: if you're contributing unequally, whether through deposit amounts, income levels, or parental gifts to just one person, joint tenancy creates profound unfairness that compounds over years.

Consider Hettie and Matthew, who bought a £280,000 flat in Bristol in 2019. Hettie put down a £20,000 deposit from her savings plus a £10,000 parental gift. Matthew contributed £5,000. They selected joint tenancy because "we're equal partners." Four years later, when they separated, the property was worth £320,000 with £240,000 remaining on the mortgage, meaning £80,000 in equity. Hettie expected to receive £30,000 of that equity (her £30,000 contribution) plus half of the remaining £50,000 (£25,000), totalling £55,000. Matthew expected a 50/50 split: £40,000 each.

Without a legal agreement specifying contribution percentages, they faced either expensive litigation or one person accepting significant financial loss. Hettie ultimately accepted £45,000 to avoid court costs, meaning she effectively gifted Matthew £10,000 of her family's money and her own savings. Had they chosen tenants in common with 60/40 ownership (reflecting their £30k vs £5k contributions) and documented it at purchase, Hettie would have received £48,000 automatically (60% of £80,000 equity), and Matthew would have received £32,000. The £3,000 difference is small, but the principle matters: proper legal structure eliminates disputes entirely.

When to choose joint tenancy:

- Equal deposit contributions and ongoing mortgage payments
- No children from previous relationships
- Strong preference for automatic inheritance to partner
- Both people have similar financial positions and risk profiles

When to choose tenants in common:

- Any unequal deposit contributions (even £5,000 difference matters)
- One person receiving parental help, the other self-funded
- Either person has children from previous relationships
- Significant income differences affecting mortgage payment capacity
- One person brings existing property equity, the other doesn't

The decision isn't reversible without cost. Changing from joint tenants to tenants in common later requires "severing the joint tenancy" through legal paperwork and potentially remortgaging if lenders won't permit it on your existing deal, costing £500-£1,500 in legal and administrative fees. Get it right at purchase.

When the Money Isn't Equal

The uncomfortable truth: equal relationship status doesn't create equal financial contributions, and pretending otherwise builds resentment that destroys partnerships silently over years.

You need a contribution tracking framework established before exchange, not after you've moved in and awkwardness has already set in. This isn't unromantic; it's protective of both people and the relationship itself.

The contribution categories that matter:

1. Initial deposit: Who contributed what amount? Include parental gifts clearly.
2. Stamp duty and purchase costs: Who paid solicitors, surveys, mortgage fees?
3. Ongoing mortgage payments: Equal split or proportional to income?
4. Maintenance and improvements: Major works like new boiler, kitchen, bathroom
5. Household running costs: Council tax, insurance, utilities (less relevant to equity, but affects financial pressure)

Rachel and Tom bought a £240,000 house in Leeds in 2021. Rachel contributed a £24,000 deposit (10%). Tom contributed £6,000 (2.5%). They chose tenants in common with Rachel owning 60% and Tom owning 40%, not matching deposit percentages exactly, but reflecting their long-term plan where Tom would contribute more to mortgage overpayments over the next five years to "equalize" to 50/50 by 2030.

They created a shared spreadsheet tracking:

- Rachel's initial deposit: £24,000
- Tom's initial deposit: £6,000
- Monthly mortgage payments: £1,100 (split £550 each)
- Tom's additional monthly overpayment: £200 (tracked separately)

By March 2024, Tom had contributed an additional £7,200 in overpayments. Their equity split had shifted from 60/40 toward 52/48, with a documented plan to reach 50/50 by late 2025. When they decided to upsize in 2025, their spreadsheet showed exact contributions, preventing any dispute about who was owed what from the sale proceeds.

The framework they used:

Contribution Type	Rachel	Tom	Notes
Initial deposit	£24,000	£6,000	Documented at purchase
Purchase costs (stamp duty, legal, survey)	£2,400	£600	Split 80/20 to match deposit ratio
Monthly mortgage payment	£550	£550	Equal split agreed
Mortgage overpayments (Mar 2021 - Mar 2024)	£0	£7,200	Tom's additional contribution
Major improvements (new boiler, 2023)	£1,500	£1,500	Split equally
Total contributions	**£27,900**	**£15,300**	**65% / 35% updated split**

This level of detail feels excessive until the relationship ends or one person wants to sell and the other doesn't. Then it becomes the only thing preventing financial destruction.

Key principles for unequal contributions:

1. Document everything from day one. A shared spreadsheet updated monthly prevents selective memory and bad faith later.

2. Separate relationship equality from financial equality. You can be equal partners in every meaningful way while acknowledging that £30,000 is more than £5,000, this is mathematics, not emotion.

3. Decide how ongoing costs affect equity. If one person pays 70% of the mortgage for five years, do they earn additional equity, or was the deposit contribution the only factor? Agree this before exchange.

4. Review annually. Contributions change as incomes change, bonuses arrive, or one person takes career breaks. An annual 30-minute review prevents drift.

5. Put it in writing. A "declaration of trust" is a legal document that sits alongside your mortgage, specifying ownership percentages and contribution rules. It costs £300-£500 and eliminates ambiguity completely.

The Conversation Nobody Wants and Everyone Needs

Planning for relationship breakdown before buying together feels like inviting failure, but it's actually the strongest protection both people can give each other.

The conversation structure that works:

Step 1: Acknowledge the discomfort directly. "This feels awkward, but we need to talk about what happens if we separate after buying. Not because I think we will, but because neither of us should be financially trapped if we do."

Step 2: Establish the facts without emotion.

- Property value: £280,000
- Mortgage remaining: £220,000
- Equity: £60,000
- Your contributions: [documented amounts]
- Ownership split: [legal percentage]

Step 3: Decide the buyout mechanics. If one person wants to stay and can afford to buy the other out:

- How is property valued? (Independent RICS valuation or average of three estate agent assessments?)
- What timeline? (60 days to decide, 120 days to complete buyout?)
- Who gets first refusal? (Person who contributed more? Person with children? Mutual agreement?)

If neither can afford to buy the other out:

- Forced sale timeline (list within 60 days, accept reasonable offers within 120 days)
- Minimum acceptable price (90% of independent valuation to prevent spite-driven underselling)
- Estate agent selection (mutual agreement or each person nominates one, third acts as tiebreaker)

Step 4: Document it legally. This conversation becomes a **deed of trust** or **cohabitation agreement** prepared by a solicitor, typically costing £500-£800. It's legally binding and eliminates every ambiguity.

Michael and Laura bought in Manchester in 2020. Their deed of trust specified:

- Ownership: 55% Michael (£22,000 deposit), 45% Laura (£18,000 deposit)
- Buyout right: Laura gets first refusal (she has a child from a previous relationship; stability matters more)
- Valuation method: Average of three estate agent assessments
- Buyout timeline: Laura has 90 days to arrange finance and buy Michael's 55% share at the agreed valuation
- Forced sale trigger: If Laura cannot buy out within 90 days, property lists for sale immediately
- Sale price floor: Neither party can reject an offer above 92% of average valuation

When they separated in 2023, the process was painful emotionally but clean financially. Three estate agents valued the property at £188,000, £192,000, and £190,000, average £190,000. Remaining mortgage: £145,000. Equity: £45,000. Laura's 45% share: £20,250. Michael's 55% share: £24,750.

Laura couldn't arrange finance to buy Michael out at £169,750 (£145k mortgage balance + £24,750 for Michael's equity). The property listed within 14 days, sold for £189,000 (above the 92% floor) within 60 days. After agent fees and solicitor costs, they each received their documented percentages of the remaining equity. No court. No dispute. No financial destruction.

The Family Money Complexity

When one person receives a £15,000 parental gift and the other is entirely self-funded, the power dynamic shifts unless you address it explicitly.

The self-funded partner often feels:

- Less entitled to decision-making despite equal ownership
- Resentful when the partner's family expresses opinions about "their" investment
- Anxious about what happens if the relationship ends and parental money cre-

ated most of the equity

The partner who received family help often feels:

- Guilty about the advantage
- Defensive when decisions are questioned
- Worried their family will be disappointed if things fail

The solution isn't avoiding parental help; it's structuring it transparently.

Option 1: Parental gift is treated as their child's contribution only. Ownership split reflects it (e.g., 65/35 if one person contributed £26,000 including gift, other contributed £14,000). Clean, but creates unequal ownership that may feel uncomfortable.

Option 2: Parental gift is treated as loan to the couple, repayable on sale. Parents draft a simple loan agreement: "£15,000 loan to Rachel and Tom, repayable upon sale of property or at our request after five years, interest-free." This is repaid before equity split, meaning both people benefit from the help equally but the parents are protected.

Option 3: Parental gift comes with explicit "no strings" documentation. Parents sign a letter: "This £15,000 is a gift to our daughter with no expectation of repayment or influence over property decisions." This prevents future disputes about whether it was a gift or loan, and removes parental claim to decision-making.

The worst option: accepting parental money with vague verbal understanding and no documentation. This creates ambiguity that explodes later.

Making Decisions Without Destroying Each Other

Joint purchase requires hundreds of decisions: which property, what offer price, which mortgage, what survey level, when to exchange, which sofa. Couples often approach this without decision frameworks, leading to paralysis (neither wants to decide), dominance (one person decides everything), or compromise that satisfies neither person.

The framework that works:

Category 1: Individual veto decisions (both must agree)

- Which property to buy
- Maximum price to offer
- Whether to proceed after survey
- Whether to exchange contracts

Category 2: Designated lead decisions (one person decides after consultation)

- Mortgage product selection (assigned to whoever has stronger financial background)
- Solicitor selection (assigned to whoever has more time to research)
- Survey level (joint discussion, one person makes final call)

Category 3: Majority rules with time limit (discuss for X minutes, then decide)

- Interior design choices
- Minor repair priorities
- Furniture purchases

Category 4: Separate domains (individual autonomy)

- Personal items in own workspace
- Own financial management
- Career decisions affecting income

This prevents the dynamic where one person feels steamrolled and the other feels progress is impossible.

The couples who navigate joint purchase successfully aren't the ones with perfect relationships or equal incomes, they're the ones who had difficult conversations before exchange, established frameworks that protect both people financially and emotionally, and treated legal structure as the foundation of partnership rather than evidence of distrust. With clear ownership agreements, transparent contribution tracking, and honest breakup planning in place, you're ready to understand how buying in London and the South East requires fundamentally different strategies than the rest of the UK, adaptations to the RENTER Framework that account for extreme price-to-income ratios while maintaining the same protection-first principles that have guided you this far.

London and South East Buyers, The Extreme Mode Playbook

London homeownership isn't impossible; it's just a different game entirely.

If you're earning £30,000–£60,000 and trying to buy in London or the South East without parental help, you already know the statistics are brutal. You've seen the price-to-income ratios that make regional cities look like a different planet. You've calculated deposits that would buy entire houses elsewhere. You've felt the sinking realisation that every strategy discussed so far needs complete recalibration for your market. This chapter exists because London and the South East require their own playbook, not because success is impossible, but because it demands adapted strategies, expanded geographic flexibility, and protection protocols that account for risks barely visible in Birmingham or Manchester.

Here's the truth you need to hear first: the RENTER Framework works in London, but it works differently.

Why London Demands a Fundamentally Different Approach

The numbers tell the story before anything else does. In Manchester, a £35,000 salary might face a 5–6x price-to-income ratio. In London, that same salary confronts 12–15x ratios as standard. A £15,000 deposit that secures a two-bedroom terrace in Leeds barely covers the fees and stamp duty on a Zone 4 one-bedroom leasehold flat.

But price differentials are only part of the equation. London's property market operates under structural conditions that don't exist elsewhere:

Property type limitations force compromises unknown in regional cities. You're not choosing between a Victorian terrace and a modern semi-detached. You're choosing between a leasehold flat with acceptable ground rent or a leasehold flat with punitive ground rent. Freehold houses at your price point exist primarily in your imagination or 90 minutes from Central London.

Leasehold dominance means 70% of London properties come with ongoing financial obligations beyond your mortgage. Service charges, ground rent, major works contributions, and lease extension costs create a second layer of housing costs that regional freehold buyers never encounter.

Post-Grenfell building safety regulations have rendered thousands of flats unmarketable and unmortgageable. The EWS1 form, a document that didn't exist before 2020, now determines whether your property has any value at all.

Transport connectivity becomes the primary value driver rather than a secondary consideration. A property 200 metres from a Tube station commands a 15–20% premium over an identical property 800 metres away. In Manchester, that distance differential might matter 3–5%.

This isn't pessimism. This is the baseline reality that your strategy must account for. The adapted RENTER Framework for London accepts these constraints as starting conditions, then builds intelligent pathways around them.

The Geographic Radius Expansion Strategy

The single most powerful adaptation for London buyers is systematic geographic flexibility, trading commute time for affordability at calculated ratios that preserve both sanity and property value.

Here's the framework that works:

Step 1: Establish Your Central Point Define where you actually need to be. Not "London" as an abstract concept, but the specific station your office sits near, or the geographic centre of your most frequent professional and social commitments. This becomes your radius origin point.

Step 2: Map Transport Corridors Identify every rail line, Tube line, and Overground route that connects to your central point. Your search area isn't a circle, it's a series of corridors following transport infrastructure. A 35-minute commute from Zone 6 on the Elizabeth Line beats a 35-minute commute from Zone 3 requiring two bus changes.

Step 3: Calculate the Affordability Gradient Research average property prices at 10-minute commute intervals moving outward from your central point. You'll typically find:

- **Zone 1–2**: £450,000–£600,000+ for one-bedroom flats (functionally inaccessible at your income)
- **Zone 3**: £300,000–£400,000 (requires 10–15% deposits = £30,000–£60,000)
- **Zone 4–5**: £220,000–£300,000 (10% deposits = £22,000–£30,000)
- **Zone 6 + Commuter Belt**: £180,000–£250,000 (10% deposits = £18,000–£25,000)

Each 10-minute commute increment typically reduces property prices by 12–18%. The question becomes: how much time are you willing to trade for how much affordability gain?

Step 4: Apply the Quality-of-Life Threshold A 75-minute each-way commute might unlock a £280,000 two-bedroom flat versus a £350,000 one-bedroom flat 30 minutes closer. But 150 minutes of daily commuting destroys quality of life, increases transport costs by £200+ monthly, and risks making you hate the property you sacrificed everything to buy. The optimal zone for most London buyers sits at 40–50 minutes door-to-desk, far enough for meaningful affordability gains, close enough to maintain professional flexibility and social life.

Step 5: Future-Proof Your Corridor Choice Crossrail (Elizabeth Line) completion transformed property values along its entire route. HS2, despite delays and political uncertainty, will eventually do the same for Euston and Old Oak Common connections. Northern Line extensions into Nine Elms and Battersea have already generated 15–20% appreciation. Your geographic expansion should favour transport corridors with confirmed infrastructure investment over corridors with stagnant connectivity.

The 30-for-30 Rule: If expanding your geographic radius by 30 minutes reduces property prices by 30%, and the location maintains strong transport links, you've found the sweet spot for London buying.

The Shared Ownership Reality Check

Shared Ownership schemes are marketed as the solution for London buyers priced out of traditional ownership. Sometimes they are. Often, they're a trap that delays full ownership by a decade while extracting maximum cost for minimum equity growth.

Here's the honest assessment no scheme provider will give you:

When Shared Ownership Makes Strategic Sense:

Condition	Why It Works
Your income is £25,000–£35,000 and traditional mortgages are genuinely inaccessible	Shared Ownership provides the only realistic entry point to London homeownership at this income level
You're buying a 50%+ initial share with clear staircasing plan to 100% within 5 years	Higher initial stakes and aggressive staircasing minimize rent payments and maximize equity capture
The property is new-build or nearly new with minimal maintenance exposure	You avoid subsidizing major works on a property you only partially own
Location is strong with confirmed transport links	Your equity share appreciates even if you never staircase to full ownership

When Shared Ownership Is a Financial Trap:

Warning Sign	Why It Fails
You're buying a 25–30% initial share on an older leasehold property	You're paying rent + service charge + ground rent + mortgage + major works contributions = potentially more than traditional ownership
Staircasing fees exceed £1,500 per transaction and you'd need 4+ staircase steps to reach 100%	The cumulative cost of staircasing erodes any initial affordability advantage
The housing association has poor reputation for maintenance and major works transparency	You're financially exposed to decisions you can't control on a property you don't fully own
Your income is £40,000+ and 10% traditional deposits are achievable within 24 months	Shared Ownership delays full ownership and costs more over 10 years than patience and larger deposits

The Shared Ownership Test: Model the total cost of Shared Ownership (mortgage + rent + service charge + staircasing fees + major works) over 10 years versus traditional ownership achieved 18–24 months later. If Shared Ownership costs less than £15,000 more over the decade, it may make sense. If it costs £25,000+ more, you're paying a premium for impatience.

Help to Buy: What It Was and What Comes Next

The Help to Buy equity loan scheme closed to new applications in March 2023, but its ghost still haunts London buyer expectations. Understanding what it provided, and what's replaced it, prevents you from waiting for government intervention that isn't coming.

What Help to Buy Delivered:

- 20% equity loans on new-build properties (40% in London)
- Interest-free for the first 5 years
- Enabled 5% deposits when 10% was standard
- Allowed buyers to access new-builds at lower income multiples

Why It's Not Coming Back: Government analysis showed Help to Buy primarily inflated new-build prices rather than increasing overall affordability. Developers simply raised prices by 15–20%, capturing the government subsidy while buyers ended up with equivalent monthly costs and higher long-term debt when equity loan repayment began.

What's Replaced It: Nothing directly. First Homes scheme offers 30–50% discounts on specific new-builds for first-time buyers earning under £80,000 (£90,000 in London), but availability is minimal and the properties come with permanent resale restrictions.

Your Strategic Response: Stop waiting for government schemes to solve London affordability. The RENTER Framework already incorporates the only scheme that matters: Lifetime ISA's 25% government bonus on savings up to £4,000 annually. That's £1,000 of free money per year, £4,000 over four years if you max contributions. It's not Help to Buy, but it's real, available, and doesn't require waiting for political decisions.

Leasehold Structures: The London-Specific Cost Reality

92% of London flats are leasehold. This isn't a problem to solve, it's a condition to understand and manage.

The Leasehold Cost Structure You Must Account For:

1. **Ground Rent**: £150–£500 annually (some legacy leases have doubling clauses that become toxic)
2. **Service Charge**: £1,200–£4,000+ annually depending on building amenities

and management quality

3. **Major Works Contributions**: £3,000–£15,000 when building requires roof replacement, lift refurbishment, or external repairs

4. **Lease Extension Costs**: £8,000–£20,000 if you buy a flat with 75–85 years remaining and need to extend to maintain value

These costs stack on top of your mortgage, council tax, and insurance. A £250,000 leasehold flat with £200/month service charge, £300 annual ground rent, and £150/month sinking fund contribution for major works costs effectively £2,150/month, versus a £1,600/month mortgage payment in isolation.

The Leasehold Evaluation Protocol:

Before making any offer on a leasehold property, demand answers to these questions:

- What's the current ground rent and are there escalation clauses?
- What's the annual service charge and its 5-year trend?
- When was the last major works bill and what's budgeted for the next one?
- How many years remain on the lease (anything under 85 years requires immediate extension planning)?
- Who's the freeholder and what's their reputation (managing agents can confirm this)?
- Are there any ongoing disputes between leaseholders and freeholder?

If the estate agent can't provide this information within 48 hours, walk. If the answers reveal ground rent doubling clauses, service charges increasing 15%+ annually, or freeholder disputes, walk faster.

The 30% Rule for Leasehold Costs: Your annual leasehold charges (service charge + ground rent + sinking fund contributions) should not exceed 30% of your annual mortgage payments. If they do, the property is financially unsustainable.

Building Safety and Cladding: Post-Grenfell Due Diligence

The Grenfell Tower fire in June 2017 exposed catastrophic building safety failures across UK housing stock. The regulatory response has created a secondary filter on

London property purchase that didn't exist before 2020: buildings must prove they're safe, or they become unmarketable.

What EWS1 Forms Actually Mean:

EWS1 (External Wall Fire Review) forms are produced by qualified fire engineers assessing whether a building's cladding poses fire risk. The form has three possible ratings:

- **A1/A2**: Building is safe, no remediation required (mortgage-able, marketable)
- **B1/B2**: Building requires remediation but interim safety measures in place (mortgage-able with caveats, marketable with disclosure)
- **Not Rated or Failed**: Building safety status unknown or confirmed unsafe (unmortgage-able, unmarketable, value = £0)

Your Protection Protocol:

1. **Before Viewing**: Ask the estate agent if the building has an EWS1 form and request a copy
2. **Before Offering**: Verify the EWS1 rating is A1/A2; anything else requires specialist advice
3. **During Conveyancing**: Confirm your mortgage lender accepts the EWS1 certificate
4. **Post-Purchase**: Understand you may face future remediation costs if government funding doesn't cover all buildings

The Buildings Safety Act 2022 established that for buildings over 11 metres, original developers bear remediation costs for buildings completed in the past 30 years. For older buildings, leaseholders can face bills of £30,000–£75,000 per flat. This isn't hypothetical risk; it's current reality affecting thousands of London leaseholders.

The Absolute Rule: Never buy a flat in a building over 11 metres without a valid EWS1 form rated A1 or A2. "Form is pending" or "remediation work scheduled" means you're purchasing a financially toxic asset that might be unsellable for 3–5 years.

Case Study: Emily's Zone 4 Success on £40,000

Emily, 31, earned £40,000 working in digital marketing at a Shoreditch agency. She'd been renting in Hackney for six years, watching prices accelerate beyond her reach while her deposit savings crawled forward. When she committed to the RENTER Framework in January 2022, she'd saved £8,000. By June 2023, 18 months later, she had keys to a one-bedroom leasehold flat in Zone 4.

Her Starting Position:

- Income: £40,000
- Existing savings: £8,000
- Student loan: Plan 2, £28,000 outstanding
- Credit score: 720 (good, not excellent)
- Maximum borrowing capacity: £180,000 (4.5x income)
- Geographic constraint: 45-minute maximum commute to Old Street

Her Adapted RENTER Framework:

(R)eveal: Emily used the Deposit Velocity Calculator and discovered she needed £22,000 for a 10% deposit on a £220,000 property, her maximum affordable price point given mortgage + leasehold costs. Current savings: £8,000. Gap: £14,000. Timeline at £400/month savings: 35 months. Unacceptable.

(E)ngineer: Emily restructured finances completely:

- Opened Lifetime ISA, contributed £4,000 immediately (£1,000 government bonus)
- Moved from Hackney (£1,100/month rent) to Edmonton (£750/month rent), accepting 15 minutes longer commute
- Cancelled £180/month of subscriptions and memberships
- Took freelance marketing work earning £400/month extra
- New monthly deposit contribution: £750 + £333 LISA = £1,083/month
- Revised timeline: 13 months to £22,000

(N)avigate: At £40,000 income, Emily's maximum mortgage was £180,000. With £22,000 deposit, she could afford properties up to £220,000. She secured Agreement in Principle at 4.8% with a high-street lender, rejecting products with early repayment charges exceeding 3% of loan value.

(T)arget: Emily mapped every Tube and Overground line reaching Old Street within 45 minutes. Her search parameters:

- **Zone 4–5 corridors**: Seven Sisters (Victoria Line), Manor House (Piccadilly), Walthamstow Central (Victoria), Leytonstone (Central)
- **Property type**: One-bedroom leasehold flat, minimum 60m^2
- **Leasehold requirements**: Ground rent under £250/year, service charge under £150/month, lease over 100 years
- **Building safety**: EWS1 form rated A1/A2 mandatory

After viewing 12 properties over 8 weeks, Emily found a 2015-build one-bedroom flat in Walthamstow, 650m from the Victoria Line station. Price: £215,000. Service charge: £1,200/year. Ground rent: £200/year. Lease: 119 years remaining. EWS1: A1 rated.

(E)xecute: Emily offered £210,000 (comparable sales supported £212,000–218,000 range). Seller countered at £213,000. Emily accepted. Survey revealed minor cosmetic issues but no structural concerns. She completed in 11 weeks.

(R)eside: Emily's monthly costs post-purchase:

- Mortgage (£191,000 at 4.8%): £1,105
- Service charge: £100
- Ground rent: £17
- Council tax (Band C): £140
- Buildings insurance: £25
- **Total**: £1,387/month

This compared to her previous £1,100/month rent, representing a £287 monthly increase, but now building equity rather than enriching a landlord. Within six months, she'd rebuilt a £4,000 emergency fund and was overpaying her mortgage by £100/month.

What Made Emily's Strategy Work:

She accepted geographic expansion to Zone 4, adding 15 minutes to her commute but unlocking £80,000+ of affordability. She prioritized leasehold quality over property size, choosing a well-managed modern build over a larger older flat with punitive charges. She verified building safety ruthlessly, walking away from two properties with pending EWS1 forms. She compressed her timeline through aggressive income optimization rather than waiting for prices to become "more affordable."

Emily didn't buy her dream flat in Hackney. She bought a strategic entry point to London homeownership that she could afford, that met quality thresholds, and that positioned her for equity growth. Three years later, that flat has appreciated to £245,000. She's considering whether to staircase into a larger property or continue building equity in her current home.

The London market isn't impossible; it's just the extreme difficulty setting of UK homebuying. You need adapted strategies, expanded geographic flexibility, ruthless protection protocols, and realistic expectations. But the RENTER Framework, when calibrated correctly for London's unique constraints, still compresses timelines from fantasy to achievable reality. Emily's case study proves it. Now Chapter 16 will show you how regional city buyers possess structural advantages that make their journey fundamentally easier, and how to leverage those advantages without falling into the traps that affordability creates.

Regional City Buyers, Your Strategic Advantage

Regional buying isn't a consolation prize; it's a genuine competitive edge.

If you're earning £35,000 in Manchester, Birmingham, Edinburgh, Bristol, or Leeds, you possess structural advantages that London-based peers with identical salaries would surrender their Oyster cards to access. The price-to-income ratios work in your favour. The deposit timelines compress dramatically. The property quality available at your budget exceeds what London buyers can touch at twice your income. This isn't luck or circumstance; this is mathematics operating exactly as it should when geography isn't working against you. The dominant cultural narrative positions London as the centre of gravity with regional cities as secondary options for those who "couldn't hack it" in the capital. That narrative is expensive nonsense that costs believers years of unnecessary waiting and thousands in wasted rent.

Here's the truth: regional buyers executing the RENTER Framework complete 2–4 years faster than London equivalents at identical income levels.

The Numbers That Change Everything

Let's establish the baseline mathematics that separate regional markets from London/South East dynamics. These aren't projections or optimistic forecasting; these are current market realities as of 2024 that fundamentally alter what's achievable on your timeline.

Regional Price-to-Income Advantages (2024 Market Data)

City	Median Property Price	Salary Required (4.5x Multiple)	10% Deposit Required	Timeline at £300/month Savings
Manchester	£220,000	£48,889	£22,000	73 months (6.1 years)
Birmingham	£215,000	£47,778	£21,500	72 months (6 years)
Leeds	£205,000	£45,556	£20,500	68 months (5.7 years)
Bristol	£310,000	£68,889	£31,000	103 months (8.6 years)
Edinburgh	£285,000	£63,333	£28,500	95 months (7.9 years)
London	**£535,000**	**£118,889**	**£53,500**	**178 months (14.8 years)**

The table reveals the structural advantage immediately: at a £48,889 salary in Manchester, you qualify for the median property. In London, that same salary qualifies you for absolutely nothing at median prices, you'd need £118,889 just to reach the starting line. But the advantage extends beyond simple affordability. The property *type* you access in regional markets fundamentally differs from London equivalents.

What Your Money Actually Buys

In Manchester's Chorlton, Levenshulme, or Didsbury areas, £220,000 purchases a two-bedroom freehold terraced house with a garden, full ownership, no ground rent, no service charges, no lease extension anxiety. In London Zone 3, that same £220,000 might secure a studio flat on a 70-year lease with £2,500 annual service charges and impending lease extension costs exceeding £20,000. You're not comparing like-for-like properties at different price points. You're comparing entirely different asset classes.

The regional advantage operates across three distinct dimensions:

1. Freehold vs Leasehold Ownership Regional markets offer predominantly freehold houses. London forces most first-time buyers into leasehold flats with all the associated financial drains: ground rent, service charges, major works contributions, and eventual lease extension costs. A Manchester freehold means your monthly housing cost is purely mortgage and standard maintenance. A London leasehold means mortgage plus

£150–£300 monthly service charges plus £100–£200 monthly ground rent plus irregular major works bills that can hit £5,000–£15,000 without warning.

2. Space and Lifestyle Quality£220,000 in Leeds buys you two bedrooms, a garden, off-street parking, and a separate kitchen. £220,000 in London buys you a one-bedroom flat with a kitchenette and no storage. If you're planning to live in the property for 5–10 years, the quality-of-life differential compounds daily. Garden access alone changes mental health outcomes during work-from-home periods.

3. Maintenance Cost Predictability Freehold ownership means you control maintenance timing and contractor selection. Leasehold means you're billed for works you didn't approve at prices you can't negotiate. Regional buyers escape the leasehold maintenance lottery entirely.

The Regeneration Assessment Framework

Not all regional cities offer identical investment fundamentals. Transport connectivity, devolution funding, and regeneration pipeline create substantially different appreciation trajectories. You need to assess where your chosen city sits on the growth curve before committing capital.

Transport Infrastructure as Appreciation Predictor

The single most reliable medium-term appreciation indicator for regional properties is planned transport infrastructure investment. HS2 routes, tram extensions, and enhanced rail connectivity don't just improve commute times, they fundamentally revalue entire neighbourhoods by compressing journey times to employment centres.

Birmingham's HS2 completion will compress London commutes to 49 minutes, closer than many current London Zone 5–6 residents currently experience.

The framework for assessing regeneration potential:

1. Confirmed Transport Investment (Not Speculation) Only count infrastructure with confirmed funding and construction timelines. "Potential future tram extension" means nothing. "HS2 station opening 2026 with confirmed £800 million adjacent development" means everything. Check local authority planning portals for approved major developments, not newspaper speculation.

2. Devolution Funding Allocation Cities with devolved mayoral authorities controlling substantial budgets (Manchester, Birmingham, West Yorkshire) demonstrate faster regeneration execution than cities dependent on central government approval for every initiative. Greater Manchester's £1.2 billion Affordable Homes Programme and

£160 million Brownfield Land Fund create predictable development pipelines that drive appreciation in targeted zones.

3. University and Knowledge Economy Presence Cities with expanding university sectors and knowledge economy employers (Manchester's MediaCityUK, Edinburgh's tech corridor, Birmingham's HS2 growth zone) generate sustained rental demand and owner-occupier markets even during economic downturns. Check graduate retention rates, cities keeping 40%+ of graduates create sustained demand.

4. Neighbourhood-Level Indicators Within cities, assess specific areas using these signals:

- **Landlord-to-owner ratios**: Areas shifting from 60%+ landlord ownership to 50%+ owner-occupier show strengthening fundamentals
- **Planning approval patterns**: Approved developments converting commercial to residential indicate confidence in area trajectory
- **Transport accessibility**: Properties within 15-minute walk of train stations with direct city centre access appreciate 15–20% faster than equivalent properties requiring bus connections
- **School catchment trajectories**: Ofsted rating improvements in local primaries precede family buyer influx by 18–24 months

The Remote Work Calculation

The post-pandemic normalisation of hybrid and remote work fundamentally rewrites the regional buyer equation. Previously, regional affordability came with a career penalty, accepting lower salaries or slower progression in exchange for property access. That trade-off no longer exists for knowledge workers in many sectors.

If you're earning a London-equivalent salary while working remotely from Manchester, Birmingham, or Leeds, you've unlocked a combination impossible for previous generations: top-quartile income with regional cost structure. The numbers become extraordinary.

London Salary + Regional Costs = Compressed Timeline

A £50,000 software developer role now pays identically whether you're in Shoreditch or Sheffield. But the property equation changes completely:

- **London scenario**: £50,000 salary, £535,000 median property, £53,500 deposit required, 178-month timeline at £300/month savings

- **Manchester scenario**: £50,000 salary, £220,000 median property, £22,000 deposit required, 73-month timeline at £300/month savings

You've compressed the timeline by 105 months, nearly 9 years, purely through geographic arbitrage while maintaining identical career trajectory and earning potential.

The calculation you need to run:

1. Verify Permanent Remote/Hybrid Status Confirm your role is contractually remote or hybrid, not temporarily pandemic-adjusted with planned return-to-office. Check whether your employment contract specifies location flexibility or whether it's informal arrangement subject to policy reversal.

2. Assess In-Person Requirement Frequency If your role requires monthly or quarterly London presence, calculate the annual cost of train travel against the property savings. Manchester–London return is £150–£200 on advance purchase. Twelve trips annually cost £2,400. You're still £15,000+ better off annually on reduced housing costs even after factoring travel.

3. Career Progression Implications Honestly evaluate whether physical absence from headquarters limits promotion potential in your specific organization. Some companies operate genuinely location-blind promotion processes. Others still favour proximity despite remote-work policies. If career ceiling exists, quantify it: is a potential 10–15% salary reduction over 5 years worth £100,000+ in housing cost savings and 9-year timeline compression? For most buyers, the answer is unambiguously yes.

4. Lifestyle Preference Audit Remote work enables regional living only if you actually want to live regionally. If your identity and social network are deeply London-embedded, the affordability advantage becomes irrelevant because you'll be miserable. This decision requires genuine honesty about whether you're choosing regional living strategically or accepting it reluctantly.

The Over-Buying Trap

Regional affordability creates a distinct danger absent from London markets: purchasing beyond genuine need because properties feel "cheap" relative to London-conditioned expectations. This trap converts your structural advantage into financial vulnerability through excess maintenance burden, heating costs, and opportunity cost locking capital in underutilized space.

When you can buy a four-bedroom detached house in Leeds for £280,000, the price of a London one-bedroom flat, the temptation to maximize square footage becomes overwhelming. Resist it unless your actual household composition and 5-year plan justify the space.

The Three Over-Buying Scenarios

Scenario 1: The Speculative Upsizer You're currently single or a couple without children, but you purchase a three- or four-bedroom house because "we might have kids eventually" or "it's good investment to have extra space." The additional bedrooms sit empty for 3–5 years while you pay:

- £800–£1,200 additional annual heating costs for unused rooms
- £200–£400 annual council tax premium for larger property band
- £150–£300 annual maintenance costs for additional bathrooms, roof area, garden space
- Opportunity cost: the £40,000 additional purchase price could generate £2,400 annually in index fund returns

Total annual cost of empty bedrooms: £3,000–£5,000. Over 5 years before hypothetical children arrive, you've spent £15,000–£25,000 heating and maintaining space you didn't use.

Scenario 2: The Ego Buyer You buy the biggest property your mortgage approval allows because it signals success to peers and family. A £60,000 salary qualifies you for £270,000. You could buy a perfect two-bedroom terraced house for £200,000, leaving £70,000 borrowing capacity and lower monthly payments. Instead, you maximize the mortgage to buy a three-bedroom semi-detached at £270,000 because it "looks better." You've added:

- £315 additional monthly mortgage cost (£70,000 at 4.5% over 25 years)
- £100 additional monthly maintenance reserve
- £60 additional monthly utility costs

Total: £475 monthly (£5,700 annually) for aesthetic signalling. That's £28,500 over 5 years that could have rebuilt your emergency fund, funded career development, or generated investment returns.

Scenario 3: The Maintenance Under estimator You purchase a period property or fixer-upper because the purchase price feels like a bargain at £180,000 versus £220,000 for modern equivalents. You underestimate the annual maintenance requirement for pre-1920s housing stock:

- £2,000–£4,000 annually for older heating systems, roof repairs, window maintenance
- £1,500–£3,000 for periodic replastering, damp treatment, external painting
- £500–£1,000 for higher insurance premiums on non-standard construction

The "bargain" £180,000 purchase costs £4,000–£8,000 annually more in maintenance than the £220,000 modern alternative. Over 10 years, you've spent £40,000–£80,000 extra, eliminating the purchase price advantage entirely while enduring constant maintenance disruption.

The Right-Sizing Framework

Purchase based on your current household composition plus confirmed 2-year horizon, not speculative 5-year fantasy:

- **Solo buyer**: Two-bedroom maximum unless you run a genuine home business requiring dedicated office space
- **Couple without children**: Two-bedroom terrace or flat, upgrading later if family actually arrives
- **Couple with one child or confirmed pregnancy**: Three-bedroom house
- **Couple with two+ children**: Three- or four-bedroom house based on children's ages and separate room requirements

If you're solo or a couple without children and you're considering three+ bedrooms "for future flexibility," you're over-buying. Sell and upgrade when the household composition actually changes, you'll benefit from appreciation on the smaller property and avoid years of wasted heating and maintenance costs.

Case Study: Sarah, Manchester, £35,000 Salary, 14-Month Completion

Sarah earned £35,000 as a marketing coordinator at a Manchester tech company. She'd been renting in Fallowfield for six years, spending £725 monthly on a one-bedroom flat and watching the deposit goalposts move further away despite consistent £250 monthly savings. She discovered the RENTER Framework in January 2023 with £9,000 already saved. Fourteen months later, in March 2024, she completed on a two-bedroom terraced house in Levenshulme for £185,000.

Stage 1: Reveal (Months 1–2)

Sarah's complete financial audit revealed £35,000 gross salary (£2,150 monthly net), £725 rent, £180 student loan, £140 car finance, £90 phone and subscriptions, £200 food, £150 transport, £100 social, leaving £565 monthly discretionary. She had £9,000 saved in a standard savings account earning 0.5% interest.

Her Millennial Buyer Matrix profile: solo buyer, regional city (Manchester), £35,000 income. Her maximum mortgage at 4.5x salary: £157,500. Adding her target £18,500 deposit (10% of £185,000 target property) gave her maximum property price of £176,000. The Deposit Velocity Calculator showed she needed £9,500 additional deposit, achievable in 14 months at £680 monthly savings, requiring her to increase from £250 to £680, a £430 monthly increase.

Stage 2: Engineer (Months 3–6)

Sarah opened a Lifetime ISA in February 2023, depositing £4,000 immediately (receiving £1,000 government bonus by April 2024). She restructured her discretionary spending: cancelled Netflix and Spotify (£20 monthly), switched phone contract to SIM-only (£25 monthly saving), reduced social budget from £100 to £50 (£50 monthly), moved car insurance to annual payment (£15 monthly saving), and eliminated impulse clothing purchases (£80 monthly average). Total monthly savings increase: £190.

She picked up freelance social media work for two local businesses at £240 monthly additional income. Combined with spending cuts, she now saved £680 monthly automatically transferred to her Lifetime ISA on payday.

Stage 3: Navigate (Months 7–8)

Sarah used a whole-of-market broker who secured an Agreement in Principle at 4.3% fixed for 5 years with 10% deposit requirement. Her maximum mortgage: £157,500. Combined with her projected £18,500 deposit by Month 14 (£13,500 saved + £4,000 LISA + £1,000 government bonus), her maximum property price: £176,000. She set her Rightmove search parameters at £165,000–£185,000 for two-bedroom terraced houses in Levenshulme, Burnage, and Gorton.

Stage 4: Target (Months 9–12)

Sarah viewed fourteen properties over eight weeks, applying the Property Intelligence Filter rigorously. She rejected eleven properties for various red flags: damp evidence, poor EPC ratings, proximity to major roads, or structural concerns flagged by her surveyor father's informal walk-throughs. Three properties met all criteria. She focused on a two-bedroom terrace in Levenshulme listed at £185,000.

Stage 5: Execute (Months 13–14)

Sarah offered £180,000, citing comparable sales and 98-day listing period. The seller countered at £183,000. Sarah held at £182,500, her maximum comfort level, and the seller accepted. Survey revealed minor roof repairs required (£1,200). Sarah renegotiated to £181,500 final price, with the seller agreeing to complete repairs pre-completion.

She exchanged in February 2024 and completed in March 2024, fourteen months after starting the RENTER Framework. Her monthly mortgage payment: £850 (versus £725 rent), leaving her £300 monthly for maintenance reserve and emergency fund rebuilding.

Key Decisions Sarah Made Correctly

1. **Stayed solo**: Didn't wait for a partner or assume future relationship would materialize

2. **Right-sized**: Purchased two-bedroom terrace, not three-bedroom semi, keeping payments manageable

3. **Negotiated hard**: Used days-on-market data to secure £3,500 reduction from asking price

4. **Accepted 10% deposit**: Didn't wait to save 15–20%, understanding mortgage approval is achievable at 10% with strong credit profile

5. **Prioritized location fundamentals**: Levenshulme offered direct tram access to city centre (18 minutes), planned regeneration investment, and strengthening owner-occupier ratio

Sarah's timeline: 14 months from framework start to completion. Her London-based university friends earning identical salaries remained renters, still 8–10 years from deposit readiness at London prices.

The Transport Infrastructure Advantage You're Not Pricing In

Regional buyers accessing transport connectivity improvements benefit from appreciation accelerators that London completed generations ago. When HS2 reaches Birmingham journey times to London compress to levels that redefine "commutable" for high-value roles requiring occasional office presence.

The appreciation pattern follows infrastructure delivery by 18–36 months. Properties within 1km of HS2 stations in Birmingham's Curzon Street area have already appreciated 25–30% since route confirmation. You're not buying property in cities waiting for investment, you're buying in cities where £96 billion of confirmed transport infrastructure is actively under construction, with completion timelines creating predictable appreciation catalysts.

How to Position for Infrastructure Gains

1. **Buy within 15-minute walk of confirmed stations**: HS2, tram extensions, or rail line improvements

2. **Prioritize routes offering sub-90-minute London access**: Opens higher-salary remote roles requiring quarterly presence

3. **Check planned development adjacent to stations**: Council-approved schemes indicate professional confidence in area trajectory

4. **Avoid speculative corridor pricing**: Buy properties that work for your current life, with infrastructure appreciation as bonus, not primary rationale

You're Not Compromising, You're Winning

Regional city buyers executing the RENTER Framework aren't accepting second-best, you're accessing the only remaining UK property markets where the mathematics still work for first time buyers without parental help. London's price-to-income ratios have broken completely. Regional cities offer the last functioning version of homeownership as your parents understood it: achievable through income and savings alone.

Your advantage is structural, not temporary. Your timeline is compressed, not aspirational. Your property quality exceeds what London equivalents can access at any price point reasonable for your income bracket. The knowledge separating successful regional buyers from those who waste their advantage through over-buying or misplaced insecurity is now yours.

In the next chapter, we'll confront the scenarios that break even well-executed plans: job loss, relationship breakdown, health crises, and interest rate shocks. Regional buyers aren't immune to life disruptions, but you can build resilience that keeps your property when everything else falls apart.

When the Plan Breaks, Resilience Strategies for Life Disruptions

The homebuyers who keep their properties through the worst years aren't the ones who earned the most, they're the ones who prepared the most.

That sentence might feel uncomfortable to read right now, especially if you've spent the last twelve months focused entirely on getting *onto* the ladder. But here's the truth that most first-time buyer guides quietly skip past: completion is not the end of financial risk. In many ways, it's the beginning of a new kind of it. Your mortgage is now a fixed obligation. Your emergency fund has likely taken a hit. And for the first time, the consequences of a job loss, a health crisis, or a relationship breakdown extend well beyond next month's rent.

This chapter isn't designed to frighten you. It's designed to make sure that when life disrupts your plan, and at some point, it will, you have a structured response waiting, not a panic. The buyers who lose their homes rarely do so because they made one catastrophic decision. They lose them because they were unprepared for a disruption they never planned for, and they ran out of road before they found their footing.

You won't be one of them.

When Your Income Drops or Disappears

Redundancy is the disruption most homeowners fear but fewest prepare for. If you lose your job or experience a significant income reduction, **the single most costly mistake**

you can make is silence. Lenders are not your enemy in this scenario, but they become significantly less flexible once arrears have already developed.

The moment your income is threatened, your action sequence is this:

1. **Activate your mortgage payment protection insurance** if you have it. Check your policy terms at once, most have a 30–90 day waiting period before payments begin, which means the clock starts the day you let them know, not the day you apply.

2. **Contact your lender directly and proactively**, before you miss a payment. Most major UK lenders offer mortgage forbearance options, temporary payment holidays, interest-only switches, or term extensions, but these are significantly easier to access when you approach them before arrears begin.

3. **Trigger your emergency fund deliberately, not gradually.** Don't nibble at it. Calculate exactly how many months of full mortgage coverage your fund provides, then work backwards to your job search timeline. This converts fear into arithmetic, and arithmetic is manageable.

The table below shows how different emergency fund sizes translate into runway at common mortgage payment levels:

Monthly Mortgage	3-Month Fund	6-Month Fund	12-Month Fund
£800	£2,400	£4,800	£9,600
£1,000	£3,000	£6,000	£12,000
£1,200	£3,600	£7,200	£14,400
£1,500	£4,500	£9,000	£18,000

This is why the six-month target isn't arbitrary. At £1,000 per month, a three-month fund gives you twelve weeks. A six-month fund gives you twenty-four. That added time is often the difference between a measured job search and a desperate one.

Relationship Breakdown After a Joint Purchase

No one buys a home expecting to need a withdrawal plan. But if you bought jointly and your relationship ends, the legal and financial reality moves fast, and feelings, however valid, don't pause the mortgage.

Your three options in a joint ownership breakdown are:

- **One partner buys out the other.** This requires a formal valuation, agreement on the equity split, and a full remortgage in the remaining partner's sole name. The buying-out partner must prove they can service the mortgage alone.

- **Both parties agree to sell.** The cleanest resolution financially. Proceeds are distributed according to the ownership structure, joint tenants split equally, tenants in common split according to the declared shares.

- **Forced sale via court order.** If you can't agree, either party can apply to the courts under the Trusts of Land and Appointment of Trustees Act 1996 (TOLATA) to compel a sale. This is slow, expensive, and should be the absolute last resort.

If you bought as tenants in common with a Declaration of Trust reflecting unequal contributions, which Chapter 14 strongly recommended, this document becomes your protection. It clearly defines who contributed what, and it holds legal weight in any dispute.

The most painful version of this scenario is the one where neither party can afford the property alone and neither wants to sell. There's no elegant answer here, but there is a practical one: get a solicitor involved early, agree a timeline for a sale decision, and separate your emotions about the relationship from your decisions about the asset. The property doesn't know you're heartbroken. It just needs managing.

Health Crises and Caring Responsibilities

A serious illness or a sudden caring responsibility, an aging parent, a child with added needs, can reduce your working hours, your income, or both, often with little warning.

The financial adaptations available to you include:

- **Statutory Sick Pay (SSP)** covers up to 28 weeks, currently paying £116.75 per week. If your mortgage is £1,000 per month, SSP alone won't cover it. Your emergency fund is the bridge.

- **Income protection insurance**, if you have it, kicks in after a deferred period and replaces a part of your salary, typically 50–70%. If you don't have it yet, this chapter is your prompt to get it.

- **Mortgage payment holidays** stay available through most lenders for borrowers in genuine hardship, though they extend your term and increase total interest paid. They are not free, but they are far cheaper than arrears.

The practical truth is this: **caring responsibilities are the most under planned disruption in personal finance**. Most people address job loss, fewer address health, and almost no one plans for becoming a carer. If there is someone in your life whose health could change your working situation, build that scenario into your resilience thinking now.

Interest Rate Shock at Remortgage

If you fixed your mortgage rate for two or three years during a period of low interest rates, you may face a materially different rate environment when your deal expires. This is not a failure. It is a known risk of fixed-rate products, and it's manageable if you prepare for it.

Start your remortgage research six months before your current deal ends. This gives you time to lock in a product offer (most are valid for three to six months), implement any final credit improvements, and avoid rolling onto your lender's Standard Variable Rate, which is always significantly higher than available fixed deals.

The decision framework at remortgage is straightforward:

Scenario	Recommended Action
Rates higher, equity increased	Consider shorter fix to receive help from future rate reductions
Rates higher, equity unchanged	Prioritise lowest available rate, extend term if needed to keep payments manageable
Rates lower than current fix	Assess early repayment charge versus saving on lower rate, calculate break-even point
Significant overpayments made	Confirm you're in a lower LTV band and use this to access better rates

The one thing you should never do is nothing. Rolling onto a standard variable rate (SVR) passively costs the average UK homeowner £2,000–£4,000 per year. Your remortgage is not a bureaucratic inconvenience; it's one of the highest-value financial decisions you'll make as a homeowner.

Property Value Decline and Negative Equity

If your property value falls below your outstanding mortgage balance, you're in negative equity. The first thing to understand is this: **negative equity only becomes a crisis if you need to sell or remortgage at that moment.** If you're staying put and servicing your mortgage, it is a number on a spreadsheet, not an emergency.

The strategic responses available to you depend on your circumstances:

- **If you can stay**, stay. UK property values have historically recovered over medium-term holding periods. The owners who crystallised losses in 2009 or 2020 did so because they were forced to sell, not because they wanted to.

- **If you need to remortgage**, contact your lender about a product transfer. Many lenders will allow existing customers to move to a new fixed rate without requiring a formal revaluation, preserving your options without exposing you to the valuation problem.

- **If you genuinely cannot service the mortgage**, contact your lender before arrears develop. Voluntary agreements, including assisted voluntary sales, are far less damaging to your credit file than repossession.

The psychological weight of negative equity is often heavier than the financial reality. Separate the two. The question is never "what is my home worth today?" The question is "can I service this mortgage, and do I need to sell?" If the answer to the first is yes and the second is no, you're fine.

Your Emergency Fund Is Your Insurance Policy

After going through every disruption scenario above, one thread connects all of them: the emergency fund is not a nice-to-have. It is the mechanism that converts every crisis from a forced sale into a managed recovery.

Three months is the floor. It's the minimum you need to avoid arrears in a short-term income disruption. But every buyer who has lived through a real disruption, redundancy, health crisis, relationship breakdown, will tell you the same thing: **six months is where genuine security begins**.

The Emergency Fund Rebuild Protocol introduced in Chapter 11 gives you the month-by-month framework to get there within your first year of ownership. If you're reading this before you've started that rebuild, start now. If you're reading this after a disruption has already hit, rebuild it as your first financial priority once stability returns, before overpaying your mortgage, before holidays, before anything.

The Buyer Who Lost Their Job in Month Eight

In early 2022, a 34-year-old project manager in Bristol, we'll call her Priya, completed on a two-bedroom flat with a £187,000 mortgage. Eight months later, her employer announced a restructure. She was made redundant with six weeks' notice.

Priya had a four-month emergency fund. She had mortgage payment protection insurance with a 60-day deferred period. And critically, she contacted her lender within two weeks of her redundancy, not after she'd missed a payment.

Her lender agreed to a three-month interest-only period while her protection insurance claim was processed. Her monthly outgoing dropped from £940 to £480. She found a new role eleven weeks later, a slight pay increase on her previous salary. She never missed a mortgage payment. Her credit file was untouched.

What saved Priya wasn't luck. It was four decisions she made *before* the redundancy: building the emergency fund, taking out income protection, contacting her lender proactively, and knowing exactly what levers to pull in which order. The Renter Liberation System doesn't end at completion. It continues exactly for moments like this.

The Six-Month Target Is the Standard

After reading these scenarios, the logic behind six months of emergency reserves should feel less like cautious advice and more like structural necessity. Three months covers a short disruption. Six months covers a serious one, with enough runway to make good decisions rather than desperate ones.

Every resilient homeowner you'll ever meet, the ones who came through redundancy, illness, break-ups, and rate shocks with their property intact, built their resilience architecture *before* they needed it. That's not a coincidence. That's the system working.

You're not reading this because you're expecting disaster. You're reading it because you're building something worth protecting.

Having built the resilience architecture that protects your homeownership through whatever life delivers, the final chapter shifts from protection to pride, exploring the full arc of what you've achieved, what it means for your future, and how the knowledge you've built can become the foundation for everything that comes next.

From Homeowner to Mentor, Consolidating Your Transformation

> The person who sat up at 2am scrolling Rightmove, convinced the whole system was designed to keep them out, is not who you are anymore.

That version of you, anxious, overwhelmed, quietly ashamed of still renting, made decisions based on fear and incomplete information. You researched obsessively and felt worse for it. You watched peers receive parental deposits and wondered whether you were simply naive to keep trying. You carried the weight of a goal that felt perpetually out of reach, and you carried it alone. That was not weakness. That was the entirely rational response of an intelligent person navigating a system that gave them almost nothing to work with.

But here you are. On the other side.

You know what an AIP is and how to get one in the top quartile of available rates. You can walk into a viewing and identify leasehold red flags before the estate agent has finished their introduction. You understand your Millennial Buyer Matrix profile, your deposit velocity, your mortgage product options, and your legal protections. You did not inherit that knowledge. You built it, systematically, one structured step at a time.

This chapter is about making sure you know that, and know what to do with it next.

Stop and Name What You've Actually Done

Most people rush straight from completion into the next project without pausing to acknowledge the distance they have covered. Do not do that.

The gap between where you started and where you stand now is not just financial. Yes, you have built a deposit, secured a mortgage, and legally transferred property into your name. But the more significant shift is this: **you now understand a system that the majority of people your age find genuinely impenetrable.** You navigated the mortgage market, read a survey report, coordinated a solicitor, negotiated an offer, and reached completion, without a parental buffer, without a safety net, and without anyone handing you the answers.

That is a different kind of achievement to what it looks like on the surface. The keys are the visible proof. The knowledge is the actual prize.

Take a moment, seriously, set the book down if you need to, and acknowledge what you have proved. Not to Instagram. Not to your parents. To yourself.

Helping Others Without Losing Yourself

Within weeks of completing, it will happen. A friend, a colleague, a cousin will find out you have bought, and they will start asking questions. At first, it feels good, you're the person who figured it out. But without a clear framework for how you share what you know, that goodwill can quietly curdle into resentment.

Here is the approach that works:

1. Give your time once, generously. Offer one focused conversation, a coffee, a call, an hour, where you walk them through the RENTER Framework at a high level. Cover the stages, the common mistakes, and the mindset shift. Do it wholeheartedly. Then point them toward the right resources and let them do their own work.

2. Refer, do not replace. You are not a mortgage broker, a solicitor, or a financial adviser. When questions go beyond your direct experience, refer them to the professionals who can actually protect them. Saying "I used a broker called X and they were excellent" is more valuable, and more honest, than attempting to answer a question outside your lane.

3. Protect your energy by design. You can care about someone's homebuying journey without being on-call for it. It is entirely reasonable to say: "I'm happy to chat through my experience, but for specific advice on your situation, you'd really benefit from speaking to a broker." That is not a brush-off. That is protecting both of you.

The goal is to share your knowledge generously without turning it into an unpaid second job. You earned what you know. You can give it away freely, on your terms.

The Thing Nobody Talks About After Completion

There is a psychological moment that catches many first-time buyers completely off guard. About four to eight weeks after completion, once the adrenaline has faded and the flat-pack furniture is assembled, a quiet question surfaces: *Is that it?*

It does not mean you made the wrong decision. It means you spent 18 months, possibly longer, with a singular, all-consuming goal, and you have now achieved it. The mental architecture you built around that goal does not disappear overnight.

What is actually happening is an **identity consolidation**. The renter who felt stuck, who carried quiet shame about their housing situation, who compared themselves to peers with parental help, that identity is dissolving. But the new one, the homeowner who got there on their own terms, has not fully settled yet. That gap is normal. It closes.

The way to move through it is to name it honestly. You proved something important. Not just to your bank or your landlord or the family members who quietly doubted whether you would manage it. You proved it to yourself. That proof is permanent. No market correction, no interest rate change, and no one else's opinion can take it from you.

What Comes Next, Without the Pressure to Decide Now

Once you are stable in your first year, emergency fund rebuilt, budget recalibrated, maintenance rhythm established, you'll naturally start thinking about what to do with the asset you have created. Here is an honest overview of the three main paths, and what each actually requires:

Path	What It Means	Best Suited For	Key Consideration
Portfolio Building	Use equity in first property to fund a buy-to-let deposit	Those with strong income growth, risk tolerance, and time to manage tenants	Requires significant equity, stress-testing, and landlord knowledge
Property Trading	Sell first property and upgrade strategically as equity and income grow	Those planning life changes, family, relocation, career moves	Timing, stamp duty costs, and capital gains implications matter
Optimise Stability	Stay put, overpay mortgage, when possible, build quality of life	Those who value security, simplicity, and non-property wealth building	Often the most financially sound option for the first 3–5 years

None of these paths is inherently better than the others. The right choice is the one that aligns with your values, your life design, and your genuine financial position, not the one that sounds most impressive at a dinner party.

The biggest mistake new homeowners make at this stage is allowing social pressure to manufacture urgency. You do not need to build a property portfolio to validate your purchase. Owning one well-chosen home, living in it well, and building your life from that stable foundation is a completely legitimate, and often financially superior, strategy.

Pride That Doesn't Need an Audience

Here is something worth sitting with: homeownership was never meant to be the whole of you.

It was the goal. It was meaningful. It required real sacrifice, real discipline, and real intelligence to achieve. But it is a foundation, not a finish line. The version of you that exists beyond this achievement, the person who knows how to navigate complex systems, who can read financial documents without panic, who completed one of the most intimidating processes adult life throws at you, that person has capabilities that extend far beyond property.

Do not shrink your identity into the square footage you own. Let the achievement be what it actually is: proof of capability. Proof that you can figure out hard things. Proof that knowledge, applied systematically, is genuinely the great equaliser, even when the system is stacked against you.

The Knowledge Is Yours Now

You came to this book because you suspected the problem was not you. You were right. The information environment around UK homebuying is fractured, commercially conflicted, and designed in a way that consistently disadvantages people who do not already know the system.

You closed that gap.

Not through luck. Not through a parental deposit. Not through perfect market timing or a fortunate inheritance. Through structured knowledge, applied one stage at a time, in a sequence designed to protect you from the mistakes that derail unprepared buyers, and to compress a timeline that the prevailing narrative told you would take a decade.

The RENTER Framework does not stop being useful the moment you get your keys. Every complex, high-stakes decision you face from here, financial, professional, relational, can be approached through the same architecture: reveal your true starting point, engineer the right conditions, navigate the landscape with real information, target the right outcome, execute with protection built in, and reside in what you've built with confidence and intention.

You started this journey as someone who felt locked out.

You are the one who built the key.

The appendices that follow are your permanent reference library, the tools, templates, and resources that supported every stage of the RENTER Framework. Keep them close. Return to them when you need to. And when the friend, the colleague, or the younger sibling asks how you did it, point them to page one, because the knowledge that changed everything for you is exactly what someone else is desperately searching for right now.

Conclusion: The Keys You Earned

> The keys in your hand are not just metal, they're proof that knowledge, applied with discipline, is the most powerful force in the UK property market.

Think about where you started. The late-night Rightmove scrolling. The spreadsheets that never quite added up. The quiet, corrosive feeling that everyone else had a financial head start you were never going to close. That version of you wasn't failing. That version of you was working with a broken map in a system that had never bothered to hand you a better one. This book was the better map. And you used it.

What you've achieved isn't a transaction. It's a complete reconfiguration of how you see yourself, what you believe you're capable of, and what you now know about the most significant financial decision most people ever make. That's not a small thing. That's everything.

The Truth That Started All of This

Buying your first home was never about what you could afford. It was always about what you knew.

That sentence opened this book, and it's worth sitting with it one final time, not as a motivational line, but as a factual statement you've now personally verified. The people who remain stuck in rental properties tonight aren't stuck because their salaries are too low or their timelines too long. They're stuck because nobody handed them a structured, sequenced, protection-first system built for their exact circumstances. You had that system. You used it. The outcome followed.

This is what separates the buyers who complete from the renters who stay paralysed. It was never luck. It was never timing. And it was certainly never parental transfers. It was knowledge, organised, applied, and acted upon at each of the six critical stages that take a person from financial fog to front door.

What the RENTER Framework Actually Gave You

It would be easy to look back at the RENTER Framework as a homebuying methodology, something you used once and filed away. That would be a waste of the most valuable tool this journey produced.

What the framework actually gave you is a **repeatable operating system for high-stakes complexity**. Every time you face a decision that feels overwhelming, every time an industry seems deliberately opaque, every time you're asked to make an irreversible choice with incomplete information, the same six-stage architecture applies.

RENTER Stage	Homebuying Application	Transferable Life Application
Reveal	Financial audit and baseline	Clarify your true starting position in any challenge
Engineer	Deposit acceleration plan	Design the system before you execute the effort
Navigate	Mortgage landscape mastery	Reduce complexity to three best-fit options
Target	Property evaluation filter	Assess opportunities with criteria, not emotion
Execute	Offer, survey, completion	Act decisively at each checkpoint with protection built in
Reside	First-year homeowner stability	Consolidate the gain before pursuing the next goal

You are not just a homeowner now. You're someone who knows how to approach complexity without being consumed by it. That's a capability the UK housing market forged in you, and it belongs to you permanently.

The Future That's Now Available to You

Here's what homeownership quietly unlocks that nobody talks about during the deposit-saving years.

Financial resilience. The equity you're building isn't just a number on a Zoopla estimate. It's a buffer between you and financial crisis. It's options. It's the ability to make career decisions from stability rather than desperation, to take the risk on the new role, the freelance project, or the business idea because your housing costs are fixed and your asset is appreciating.

Career flexibility. Renters move when landlords decide. Homeowners move when opportunity calls. That's not a trivial distinction; it's the difference between a career shaped by housing availability and one shaped by professional ambition.

The compound effect of time. Every month you own rather than rent, you're building equity instead of funding someone else's portfolio. Over a decade, that difference, between the person who bought at 32 and the person who waited until 42, is measurable in tens of thousands of pounds and, more quietly, in the psychological freedom that comes from knowing your housing is secure regardless of what happens in the rental market.

The foundation for everything else. Families. Investment decisions. Community roots. The ability to paint the walls the colour you want without asking permission. None of this sounds as dramatic as it feels until you've spent a decade without it. Now you have it.

Permission to Feel Exactly What You Feel

Culture spent years telling you this wasn't possible. That the market was too expensive. That without the Bank of Mum and Dad, you were simply priced out of a generation of wealth. That renting was, for people like you, just how things were.

You can let yourself feel proud now. Not quietly. Not with caveats. **Fully and completely proud.**

Not because homeownership is the pinnacle of human achievement, it isn't, but because you did something genuinely difficult. You stayed the course through a process designed to be confusing. You made protection-first decisions when every estate agent in the chain was incentivised to rush you. You rebuilt your emergency fund when it would have been far easier to spend the relief. You arrived at completion not by accident, but by design.

The people in your life who benefited from parental deposits didn't do it wrong, they were just handed a shortcut you didn't have. You built the road yourself. That's worth acknowledging, not with arrogance, but with the quiet confidence of someone who now knows, with certainty, what they're capable of.

What You Do with This Now

There are people in your life right now, colleagues, friends, siblings, having the exact conversations you were having eighteen months ago. The 2am Rightmove sessions. The paralysing sense that the maths will never work. The quiet shame of still renting at 34.

You don't have to become an unpaid mortgage advisor. But you can share what shifted for you. Not the tactics, the mindset. The moment you understood that the information gap was the real barrier. The moment the RENTER Framework gave you a structure that converted research into action. That reframe alone is worth more than any specific tip you could pass on.

The Renter Liberation System was built to be shared, not because it benefits this book commercially, but because the information asymmetry that kept you stuck is keeping others stuck right now. Every person who escapes it through structured knowledge is one less person funding a landlord's retirement instead of their own.

Pass the map forward.

Continue building the life you designed. Revisit your financial strategy each year, your mortgage deal, your maintenance reserve, your equity position. As your circumstances change, the same RENTER principles that got you here will guide the next decision: whether that's remortgaging strategically, evaluating a second property, or simply deciding that this home serves you well for another decade and optimising around that reality.

The framework doesn't expire. Neither does the capability you've built.

The Last Thing This Book Will Ever Say to You

You were never the problem.

Not when the deposit felt unreachable. Not when the mortgage jargon was deliberately designed to confuse. Not when every property you viewed had a flaw the estate agent glossed over. Not when exchange fell through and you had to start again. Not when the people around you seemed to be progressing faster, with less effort, on foundations you weren't born with.

The information environment was broken. The system withheld the structured knowledge that would have made this journey manageable years earlier. The cultural narrative told you that homeownership without a parental gift was aspirational at best and delusional at worst.

You fixed it. With this book, with the RENTER Framework, and with the decisions you made at every stage when it would have been easier to stay stuck.

The keys in your hand are proof of that. Not just of a successful property transaction, but of what becomes possible when the right knowledge reaches the right person at the right moment.

You were always capable of this. You just needed someone to tell you the truth about what was actually standing in your way.

Now you know. And now you're home.

The companion tools referenced throughout this book, including the Deposit Velocity Calculator, the Millennial Buyer Matrix Profiler, the Mortgage Product Shortlist Filter, the Property Intelligence Filter Checklist, the Guardian Framework Decision Trees, and the Post-Purchase Financial Reset Plan, are available in the Appendices. These tools are designed to be used, shared, and returned to throughout your first year of ownership and beyond.

Appendices

The tools you hold in your hands right now are worth more than any single chapter in this book.

That might sound like an unusual thing to say at the end of a book, but it's the truth, and it matters. Everything you've read across eighteen chapters, every framework, every filter, every decision checkpoint, has been pointing towards a moment of action. Not a moment of understanding. Not a moment of inspiration. *Action.* And action requires tools. The Appendices are exactly that, the operational layer of the Renter Liberation System, translated from concept into ready-to-use instruments you can pick up and apply the morning after you finish reading. This isn't the back pages. This is where the rubber meets the road.

Think of it this way: a surgeon doesn't perform an operation armed only with medical school knowledge. They walk into the theatre with precisely calibrated instruments; each one designed for a specific task at a specific moment in the procedure. You've just completed your training. These appendices are your instruments.

Appendix A, The Companion Tool Library

Seven tools that transform strategy into action, starting today.

There's a gap that most first-time buyer books never bridge. They teach you *what* to do, then leave you alone to figure out *how*. The Companion Tool Library exists to close that gap permanently.

Each of the seven tools in this library has been built around a specific decision point in the RENTER Framework, the moments where lack of precision costs money, extends timelines, or quietly destroys confidence. These aren't supplementary materials. They are core deliverables.

1. The Deposit Velocity Calculator

This spreadsheet template is the engine behind Stage 1 (Reveal) and Stage 2 (Engineer). Input your current income, monthly expenses, existing savings, and target deposit figure, and the calculator does something no generic savings article ever will, it tells you **exactly** when you'll be ready, month by month, under different savings scenarios.

It eliminates the single most paralysing question first-time buyers carry: *"But when, actually?"* Replace the fog of "someday" with the clarity of a date. Then work backwards.

How to use it: Complete the Reveal audit in Chapter 6 first, then input your baseline figures. Revisit monthly and update when income, expenses, or savings rate changes.

2. The Millennial Buyer Matrix Profiler

Your homebuying strategy isn't the same as your colleague's, your friend's, or the person you read about in a case study. It's uniquely yours, shaped by your income, your city, and your relationship status.

The Matrix Profiler is a diagnostic tool that takes three inputs, solo or couple, London/SE or regional, income bracket, and outputs your personalised buyer profile. Each profile then directs you to the specific strategies, timelines, and scheme eligibility most relevant to your situation. Stop following generic advice. Start following yours.

3. The Mortgage Product Shortlist Filter

There are over 3,000 mortgage products available in the UK at any given time. That number is not designed to help you; it's designed to overwhelm you into accepting whatever a generalist broker or bank recommends. This filter changes that dynamic entirely.

Working through a structured decision framework across LTV band, rate type suitability, early repayment charge structure, overpayment flexibility, and arrangement fee impact, the filter reduces 3,000+ products to a shortlist of three. Three products that genuinely fit your circumstances. Three products you can take to a broker and have an informed conversation about, rather than nodding along and hoping for the best.

Use this tool in Chapter 8 (Navigate) before you seek your Agreement in Principle.

4. The Property Intelligence Filter Checklist

Emotion is the enemy of smart property decisions. You walk into a viewing, you smell the coffee the vendor has strategically brewed, you notice the light in the kitchen, and before you know it, you're mentally placing your furniture. The Property Intelligence Filter is the antidote.

This viewing template walks you through all five assessment criteria, structural integrity signals, leasehold red flags, EPC and building safety compliance, area appreciation indicators, and comparable sales benchmarking, in a structured sequence. You complete it during and immediately after every viewing. No guesswork. No selective memory. Just clean, consistent data across every property you see.

5. The Guardian Framework Decision Trees

These go/no-go decision trees are the most protection-focused tools in the library. Built around the ten catastrophic mistake checkpoints introduced in Chapter 10 (Execute), each tree guides you through a binary decision at a critical juncture, survey response, mortgage selection, contract exchange, and completion, replacing subjective judgment with structured criteria.

When you're standing at exchange, emotionally invested, sleep-deprived, and being pressured to commit, you need a process, not a feeling. The Guardian Framework gives you exactly that.

6. The Post-Purchase Financial Reset Plan

Completion day is not the finish line; it's the beginning of your most financially exposed period. Within 30 days of getting your keys, your monthly cash flow changes significantly and permanently. Mortgage payments replace rent. Council tax, buildings insurance, and contents insurance arrive. The maintenance reserve needs funding. And your emergency fund is probably depleted.

This budget template walks you through the complete financial reset: recalibrating every line of your monthly budget to reflect your new reality, allocating correctly across non-negotiable costs, and identifying where the compression needs to happen without tipping into house-poverty. Complete this tool before completion day, not after.

7. The Emergency Fund Rebuild Protocol

Your emergency fund will take a hit during the purchase process. Surveys, solicitor fees, removal costs, and immediate home essentials have a way of eroding even the most carefully protected buffer. The Emergency Fund Rebuild Protocol is a six-month savings tracker specifically designed to restore your 3-month buffer as a priority above all discretionary spending.

It includes weekly and monthly checkpoints, adjustment triggers if income or expenses change, and a simple progress dashboard so you can see the buffer growing in real time.

Rebuilding this fund isn't just financially prudent, it's psychologically essential. Knowing you have a cushion is what converts house-ownership anxiety into genuine confidence.

Appendix B, Essential Resources and Further Reading

A trusted directory of UK-specific resources, so you always know exactly where to go next.

The internet is full of first-time buyer advice. Most of it is generic, some of it is outdated, and a significant portion of it is written by people with a financial interest in the products they're recommending. This directory cuts through all of that.

Every resource listed here has been selected for one reason: it is authoritative, UK-specific, and genuinely useful at the stage indicated.

Government Schemes

- **Lifetime ISA**, GOV.UK official documentation: eligibility criteria, contribution limits, penalty rules, and first-time buyer withdrawal conditions
- **Help to Buy ISA**, guidance for those still holding active accounts (the scheme is closed to new applicants, but existing holders can still use it)
- **Shared Ownership**, GOV.UK and Homes England documentation on eligibility, staircasing rights, and resale mechanics

Credit Reference Agencies

- **Experian**, free access via the Experian app; statutory report available for £2
- **Equifax**, free access via ClearScore
- **TransUnion**, free access via Credit Karma

Check all three before applying for any mortgage product. Lenders use different agencies, a discrepancy on one report can cost you an Agreement in Principle.

Property Portals

- **Rightmove**, advanced search filters, price history by area, sold prices tool
- **Zoopla**, price estimates, area statistics, property value history
- **OnTheMarket**, frequently lists properties 24–48 hours before other portals

Mortgage Comparison and Guidance

- **MoneySavingExpert Mortgage Best Buys**, independent, updated regularly, no commercial bias

- **Which? Mortgage Advisers**, fee-free independent broker service
- **Independent mortgage broker directories**, Unbiased.co.uk and VouchedFor for vetted local brokers

Legal and Survey Bodies

- **The Law Society**, conveyancer search and quality accreditation
- **RICS (Royal Institution of Chartered Surveyors)**, accredited surveyor directory and survey type guidance
- **Homeowners Alliance**, plain-English legal and process guides for buyers

Appendix C, Glossary of UK Homebuying Terms

Every key term used in this book, defined in plain English, no jargon required.

Term	Plain English Definition
AIP (Agreement in Principle)	A provisional statement from a lender confirming how much they're likely to lend you, based on a soft credit check. Not a guarantee, but essential before making offers.
LTV (Loan-to-Value)	The percentage of a property's value you're borrowing. A £180,000 mortgage on a £200,000 property is 90% LTV. Lower LTV = better rates.
EPC (Energy Performance Certificate)	A rating from A (most efficient) to G (least efficient) showing a property's energy use. Required by law for all sales. Affects running costs and future mortgageability.
Leasehold	You own the property but not the land it sits on. A ground rent and service charge applies. Common for flats. Check lease length carefully, below 80 years is a red flag.
Freehold	You own both the property and the land. Most houses are freehold. No ground rent, no service charge, no lease countdown.
Stamp Duty	A government tax on property purchases above certain thresholds. First-time buyers have a relief that raises their nil-rate threshold. Check current rates on GOV.UK.
Conveyancing	The legal process of transferring property ownership from seller to buyer. Handled by a solicitor or licensed conveyancer.
Exchange	The point at which both parties sign identical contracts and the buyer pays their deposit to the solicitor. The deal is legally binding from this moment.

Completion	The day the remaining purchase funds are transferred, and you receive your keys. Usually 1–4 weeks after exchange.
ERC (Early Repayment Charge)	A penalty fee charged if you pay off your mortgage or switch product before the fixed term ends. Can be 1–5% of the outstanding balance.
Overpayment Flexibility	Most lenders allow you to overpay up to 10% of the outstanding balance annually without triggering an ERC. Reduces term and total interest paid.
Portability	The ability to take your existing mortgage product with you when you move, rather than having to remortgage. Useful if you're on a favourable rate mid-term.
Survey (Level 2 / Homebuyer Report)	A professional assessment of a property's condition. A Level 2 covers visible defects; a Level 3 (Building Survey) goes deeper and is recommended for older or unusual properties.
Ground Rent	An annual payment from a leaseholder to the freeholder. Post-2022 legislation restricts new ground rents to a peppercorn (effectively zero), but older leases may have escalating clauses.
Service Charge	An annual fee paid by leaseholders toward the maintenance and management of the building. Can vary significantly, always request three years of accounts before proceeding.

Appendix D, Case Study Index and Bibliography

The evidence base behind every strategy in this book, and the pathway to keep learning.

Case Study Index

Every case study featured throughout this book is drawn from real buyer journeys, with identifying details anonymised. The index below allows you to locate specific profiles quickly.

Case Study	Chapter	Profile	Outcome
Two identical incomes, 18-month timeline difference	Chapter 3	Both buyers, same city, same salary	Information access alone determined the gap
£40,000 earner completing in Zone 4 within 18 months	Chapter 15	Solo, London/SE, Shared Ownership pathway	Completion achieved through geographic strategy
£35,000 earner in Manchester completing in 14 months	Chapter 16	Solo, regional city, £15,000 deposit	Regional advantage leveraged with precision
Three solo buyers across different income levels	Chapter 13	Solo buyers, three UK cities	Distinct strategies, common framework
Two couples with different income dynamics	Chapter 14	Joint purchase, unequal contributions	Legal protection framework applied
Redundancy in Month 8 of ownership	Chapter 17	Single buyer, income disruption	Emergency protocol activated, ownership retained

Bibliography and Data Sources

- ONS (Office for National Statistics), House Price Index, regional affordability data
- UK Finance, First-time buyer lending statistics and deposit size trends
- HM Land Registry, Price Paid Data and property transaction records
- Money and Pensions Service, Financial wellbeing and debt research
- FCA (Financial Conduct Authority), Mortgage market study and consumer outcomes data
- Shelter, Private rented sector research and housing affordability analysis
- Resolution Foundation, Intergenerational wealth transfer and homeownership analysis

- Homeowners Alliance, Annual homebuying survey data

Recommended Reading

- *Richer, Wiser, Happier*, William Green
- *The Psychology of Money*, Morgan Housel
- *I Will Teach You to Be Rich*, Ramit Sethi (UK context adaptations noted in the text)
- *The Wealthy Renter*, Alex Avery (counterpoint perspective, worth engaging with critically)

You started this book as a paralysed renter drowning in contradictory information. You finish it with a complete operating system, a full tool library, and proof, drawn from real buyers at your income level, in your city, with your constraints, that this journey is not just possible. It's yours.

The keys you've earned aren't just to your front door. They're to a version of yourself that knew how, and did it anyway.

About the author

Anthony Fallon bought his first home in the UK property market without a penny of family help, and knows exactly how it feels to scroll Rightmove at 2am wondering if the maths will ever work.

As a residential building surveyor and Associate Member of the Royal Institution of Chartered Surveyors (RICS), he's spent years walking through properties other first-time buyers were about to catastrophically overpay for, watching preventable mistakes cost people years of timeline damage. He wrote this book because he got tired of watching intelligent, capable people get destroyed by information asymmetry in a system that was never designed to help them.

He lives in the North West of England, where he still remembers exactly what his own deposit runway felt like, and how good it felt to prove that knowledge beats inheritance. When not writing homebuyer surveys, he writes books on helping homebuyers.

Leave a review

If you found this book helpful in your homebuying journey please leave a review wherever you purchased the book to help others.

Many thanks,

Anthony Fallon

www.ingramcontent.com/pod-product-compliance
Lightning Source LLC
LaVergne TN
LVHW090407210926
848480LV00002B/484
* 9 7 8 1 9 1 8 1 8 9 1 1 7 *